Mirror to a Mermaid

Pictorial reminiscences of Mason College and the University of Birmingham 1875-1975

Compiled and written by Maurice Cheesewright

Published by The University of Birmingham PO Box 363 Birmingham B15 2TT England

©1975 The University of Birmingham

Printed by Suttons (Printers) Limited Birmingham

Cover Design by Gavin & Hackett Birmingham

ISBN 0 7044 0130 4   Price £2.85

INDEX

Introduction

Sir Josiah Mason laid the foundation stone of his Scientific College in Edmund Street, Birmingham, on 23 February 1875, his eightieth birthday. It was an event of greater moment than Mason or his audience knew, for it led twenty-five years later to the creation of the University of Birmingham by Royal Charter.

The College was in the plainest sense Sir Josiah Mason's, not just because it was formally so called but because he built and endowed it from his own pocket, and controlled it with the advice of a small group of private friends. In a different sense the University was Joseph Chamberlain's, not for the modest contribution he was able to make from his depleted fortune, certainly not for the idea, which had many origins, but because as Birmingham's favourite son he used his influence where power and money dwelt to found a university whose liberal constitution became a model for others.

It might have been otherwise. Birmingham might have become a junior partner with Manchester, Leeds and Liverpool in the existing Victoria Federal University; or a partner with Bristol and Nottingham in a new federal university that would have been little more than an examination board. It needed both a Mason and a Chamberlain, each in his time, to ensure that Birmingham took a straighter road to the University we know, a single corporate body committed to academic freedom and the advancement of knowledge as well as to teaching.

This book is a centenary offering. It is in no sense a pictorial history, for by that definition it must fail. Only in recent years have our photographic records been treated with any sort of respect; for instance several of those reproduced here owe their survival to Mr L Cubbin of the Finance staff who rescued them from a dustbin during the final move from Edmund Street. The material available therefore tends to be concentrated in particular subject areas or periods of time, while several major events are quite unrecorded. (The great majority of photographs, incidentally, bore no captions, so that the identification of objects, occasions and individual faces has been a major research task in itself.)

In these circumstances I have selected primarily on the basis of visual interest, using the captions to heighten interest and at the same time fill *some* of the gaps in the record, hoping that what the eye does not see the heart will not grieve for. The result is a patchwork quilt with all the failings of that homely article but also, perhaps, some of its charm.

The alternative would have been not to produce this book at all. That, I believe, would have been a pity.

M.C.

3

ACKNOWLEDGMENTS

The compilation of this book has entailed contact with more than a hundred persons and institutions, and a catalogue of them all would be rendered meaningless by its length. It is hoped therefore that those many who have helped with information and material concerning their own departments will accept a general 'thank you' which is no less warm for not being specific.

Particular thanks are due to Professor R H C Davis for enthusiastic support during the gestation period, for critical appraisal at proof stage, and for numerous helpful suggestions. It should be emphasised that the residual faults are not his but the author's.

Acknowledgement should be made of the help given by Mr T H Turner, whose father was Professor of Metallurgy 1902-26; the Rev. S A Worrall, who was a laboratory assistant at Mason College in 1895; Mr Ernest Gold, who was a student there; Dr Robert Adie and the British Antarctic Survey; the Fellows of St John's, Gonville & Caius and Trinity Colleges, Cambridge, and of Magdalen and Lincoln Colleges, Oxford; the Royal Meteorological Society; Mrs Pamela Diamand; Mr Charles Beale; Professor Neville Borg; Mrs Dorothy Styles; Miss G I M Carlier; Professor J C Robb; Mr Donald Dixon; Mr John Whybrow; the Local Studies section of Birmingham Reference Library; Miss Christine Penney and Mr Jim Davies of the University Library; Mrs Ann Giles of the Guild of Graduates, particularly for inquiries involving travel; the Editors of *The Birmingham Post*, the *Sunday Mercury* and the *Evening Mail*; Mrs I Jackson of the University House Association; Dr E T Stringer of the Edgbaston Observatory; Mr D M Lipton; Mr A Thorburn; Mr Glyn Picton; Dr B T Davis; Mr G Davies of the Estates and Buildings Office; Mr Ernest Bampton and Staff; Miss E Haydon, Dental School; Mr A Burgess; Mr R C Swift; Mr J E James; Mr R B Lockett; Mr R T Jones; Sir Arthur Thomson; Mr A Horton; Professor A L d'Abreu; Professor O Hood Phillips; Professor E D R Shearman; Mr R Barrow; Mr L Cubbin; Dr John Beal; Professor Maurice Stacey; Professor G Stacey Ward; Professor P B Moon; Miss Alice Godsell; Mr P R Middleton; Mrs F McNeille; Colonel E C Turner; Mr E R Winnall; Mrs Shaw Scott; Mr J L Mellor and Miss Helen Jones of the City Engineer's Department; Miss Gillian Hawe of *The Guildsman*; Mrs Lilian Cronne; Miss Evelyn Round; Mr E Cottam; Dr Otto Frisch; Sir Rudolf Peierls; Dr Henry Boot; Dr M R D Seaward; Mr S K Joshi; Sir Robert Aitken.

The order in which the names appear is without significance.

Erratum
p. 37 line 2 - for "three" *read* "the".

Sir Josiah's College

Josiah Mason was the archetype of a Samuel Smiles hero; his absence from the pages of *Self Help* can only be explained by his habit of anonymity. Having risen from poverty to wealth by his own industry, he gave all away to the twin causes of educating the young in self-help through science, and succouring the aged and the orphans for whom self-help offered no practical alternative to their condition.

Born in 1795, a Kidderminster carpet weaver's son, his only formal education was at a dame school and a Wesleyan Sunday school; and he tried his hand at many trades, from selling penny cakes in the streets to cobbling and weaving, before coming to Birmingham at the age of 21 to work for his maternal uncle in the gilt trinket trade. He turned an ailing business into a profitable one, and married his employer's daughter—his first cousin; but neither circumstance prevented the business being sold behind his back, so that at the age of 27 he had no job, a wife and only twenty pounds saved.

His Wesleyan connections then brought him into touch with the good Samuel Harrison, a manufacturer with an ingenious way of making split rings in a single operation. Mason took charge of the factory, with house attached, at 36 Lancaster Street, and a year later bought it for £500 in £100 instalments.

Mason's special contribution to Victorian technology was a machine-slit steel pen so excellent that it won a vast world market. This apparently simple product was the result of sixteen separate and delicate processes which included piercing, annealing, raising, hardening, scouring, grinding, polishing—and slitting, which Mason kept a close secret. When he sold out in 1875 to the London firm of Perry, who had marketed the whole of his output in earlier years under their own name, his workers numbered one thousand, and the pens in process of manufacture 90 millions, in weight 60 tons.

Among his other enterprises were silver electroplating, which he developed in partnership with the Elkington brothers, and a model village and copper works at Pembrey, South Wales. He once paid £10,000 to a struggling German inventor who used the money to found his own steel works at Essen, later becoming the first Baron Krupps.

Mason's first benefaction was a group of almshouses at Erdington for 20 women and 50 orphans; they were built and occupied without any public announcement, yet their presence revealed such a large unmet need that he conceived the idea of a bigger orphanage for 500 supported by public subscription. His first approach was to the Rector of St Martin's Parish Church, Dr Miller, who was astonished by the offer of a first contribution of £100,000 from a man of whom he had never heard, and called together a small committee.

But Mason made two absolute stipulations. The children should be taught the Holy Scriptures "as Timothy was taught", without any catechism; and there should be no distinction when selecting for admission between the "respectable" class and the "gutter" class. The gentlemen of the Church proved unyielding on both points, and Mason decided to go it alone.

He took four years building his orphanage, supervising the work himself and spending £260,000 on the structure and endowments. The public knew nothing of this until it was completed in August 1869, when there appeared in the *Birmingham Daily Post* an article written by its editor, John Thackray Bunce, who later became a trustee of Mason College. After describing the magnificent edifice Bunce wrote: "By the desire of the founder, a man of simple character and retiring habits, the event was quite unmarked by ceremony. There was just a quiet meeting of half a dozen gentlemen, the first trustees, at Mr Mason's house at Erdington."

Already Mason had begun to formulate plans for his Science College with the help of Dr J Gibbs Blake (whom he had brought to Birmingham to look after the orphans) and G J Johnson, his solicitor. For ten years Dr Blake spent his holidays studying technical colleges in Germany, France, Switzerland and the United States; later the architect, J A Cossins, made a similar tour. Blake and Johnson were appointed the first two trustees, and in 1872 four others were added: William Costin Aitken, Bunce, George Shaw and Dr Thomas Pretious Heslop. Johnson, Shaw and Heslop had all been professors in Queen's College (see later) and were evidently seeking a new home for their loyalties.

The first stone was laid on the Edmund Street site by Sir Josiah (knighted 1872) on his 80th birthday, 23 February 1875, watched by John Bright MP and a large gathering of civic representatives. He ended his little speech " . . . trusting that I, who have never been blessed with children of my own, may yet in these students leave behind me an intelligent, earnest, industrious, truth loving and truth seeking progeny." It was a day of snow and ice, and the party quickly sought the warmth of the Queen's Hotel.

Joseph Chamberlain, though Mayor of Birmingham, had excused himself on account of his first wife's recent death. He was again absent from the opening of the College in October 1880, having recently entered the Cabinet as President of the Board of Trade. Curiously, there is no record that the founder of Mason College ever met the man who was to turn it into a University.

Despite his age Mason had personally supervised the building of the College daily, on site, for five years. He employed no clerk of works. The building and endowments had cost him £200,000.

In his original deed he provided for instruction in science and medicine, without distinction of sex, class or creed, but excluded "mere literary pursuits." Before the opening he had widened this to permit an arts faculty, but remained adamant that there should be no teaching upon theology or current party political controversy.

The trustees and professors of the College dined with him on his 86th birthday, and found him in failing health. He died in his sleep four months later and was buried alongside his wife in a mausoleum in the Orphanage grounds. At a simple ceremony in the Orphanage chapel those present received a memorial card bearing these texts:

> I delivered the poor that cried, and the fatherless, and him that had none to help him—JOB XXIX 12
> By the blessing of the Lord I profited, and filled my winepress like a a gatherer of grapes. Consider that I laboured not for myself only, but for all them that seek learning—ECCLESIASTICUS XXXIII 16

This full-length portrait of Sir Josiah Mason was completed in 1872 by Henry Turner Munns, a member of the Royal Birmingham Society of Artists. Pen and open cheque book are evident symbols of the sitter's public generosity. A group of private subscribers commissioned the picture and presented it to Birmingham Town (not yet City) Council for hanging in the Art Gallery.

It is now on loan from the City Museum and Art Gallery to the University and hangs in the Senate Room, behind the Chairman's seat.

Mason's executors subsequently commissioned from the same artist a half-length replica which hung in the board room of Mason College and is still in the University's possession.

Erdington,
Birmingham. Decr 10. 1870.

My dear Mr Thos. Avery

By a codicil to my will
dated the 8th of December I have
given to you absolutely some freehold
and leasehold property in Lancaster
Street Princip Street Cleveland Street
Steelhouse Lane Edmund Street and
Great Charles Street — The two
latter properties I intend for the site
of a College and Schools for technical
education and instruction and the
other properties towards the endowment
for which I intend to make further
provision by my will.

The object and purpose of the
Institution are fully detailed in a
trust deed which I hope shortly to
execute, but in case of my death
before such deed can be perfected
according to the statute of mortmain
I have given this property to you in
full confidence that you will
deal with it as I should have done
if living.

I am my dear Mr Thos. Avery
faithfully yours
Josiah Mason

Josiah Mason's orphanage at Erdington, engraved from a photograph by Thomas Lewis the Birmingham photographer. It was built to accommodate up to 500 children. The equipment included a steam-heating system and a baking oven both of which Mason designed. Behind it stood Mason's earlier benefaction—a row of buildings to accommodate 20 elderly women and 50 orphans. In recent years the trustees decided that the building did not conform with the modern principle of providing foster homes for small groups of orphans; it was pulled down and the site sold for housing. The endowments now support three old people's homes in Erdington, Olton and Shirley.

The trust deed by which Mason College was established and endowed was signed by the founder in December 1870, but by the Statute of Mortmain it would have become null and void if Mason had died in the ensuing 12 months. To provide against this eventuality he executed a codicil to his will leaving the endowment properties absolutely to Thomas Avery, thrice Mayor of Birmingham, and at the same time he wrote this letter which was to be handed to Avery should the need arise. In this he was advised by his great friend and legal adviser Mr George J Johnson, who had been Professor of Law in Queen's College, Birmingham. The letter was handed to the University by his nephew Mr Edward Johnson the Birmingham solicitor.

A portrait of Avery now hangs in the Crown public house, Broad Street, near the new Repertory Theatre.

Mason's Science College Birmingham

J·A·Cossins Architect

This sketch design for Mason College was completed some time before 1876— probably for the stone-laying on 23rd February 1875. *The Architect* reported that "Professor Roscoe, than whom no man in England has more opportunities of studying plans, arrangement, and fittings of scientific institutions, has said that the Mason College is as complete and perfect for the purposes required as any building in this Country or on the Continent". The Municipal Reference Library in Ratcliff Place (left) had already been built, but the handsome globular street lamps, the marble statue of Mason seated, the Chamberlain Memorial and Fountain still lay in the future.

The style was described as 13th century with "details of a somewhat French character". For the frontage "an excellent deep red brick from Kingswinford has been employed, with Portland, Bath and Bolton Wood stone for the windows and other details". Heating and cooling were effected by means of ducts which drew air over a coil of steam-heated pipes.

This contemporary sketch (LEFT) in the London *Graphic* showed Sir Josiah Mason, then in his 86th year, receiving guests at the conversazione in the physics laboratory of his new College on the opening day, 1 October 1880. Standing on the dais with the key in his hand he said: "The key of my College is now mine, and I can say that the College is mine; but in a moment I shall be able to say so no longer, for I now present it, and with it the College, to my old friend, Mr Johnson, on behalf of my trustees, to be held by them in trust for the benefit of generations to come".

It was the culmination of a day of celebration which had begun that morning with a meeting in the Town Hall, presided over by the Mayor of Birmingham and attended by representatives of the corporations of Birmingham and Kidderminster, the leading scientific and literary institutions of Birmingham, the universities of Oxford, Cambridge and London and the Victoria Federal University (Leeds, Liverpool and Manchester). The Birmingham Festival Choral Society sang Mendelssohn's hymn *Let our theme of praise ascending*, and the opening address was delivered by Thomas Henry Huxley who pleaded for arts subjects to be added to the curriculum—also sociology.

This pre-1886 photograph of Mason College shows how municipal pride had burgeoned in Ratcliff Place since the College was first planned. In the centre is the memorial erected in 1876 as a tribute to Joseph Chamberlain, who had retired from municipal affairs on entering the House of Commons; it is still there. To the left is the marble statue of Mason seated, holding the College foundation deed in his hand, for which funds were raised at a public meeting after his death—and to which 30 years later Sir Oliver Lodge despatched a porter with instructions to "remove at once the small boy sitting on Sir Josiah's knee". The statue has gone but a bronze casting of the head and shoulders has been erected at Erdington. The memorial on the right is to George Dawson, a widely renowned preacher and populariser of Shakespeare, and an early advocate of free public libraries and secular schools.

William Sands Cox

William Sands Cox (ABOVE) was the true father of the Birmingham School of Medicine. In 1825 he began a series of lectures on anatomy in the house of his father, a Birmingham surgeon, at 24 Temple Row. In 1836 William IV conferred upon it the title of the Birmingham Royal School of Medicine and Surgery, later changed by Queen Victoria to Queen's College. An 1889 photograph of the College building in Paradise Street is on the opposite page.

Under Cox's dynamic influence was also established the Queen's Hospital as a teaching adjunct of the College; the original building, much changed, is now the Accident Hospital in Bath Row. The College acquired faculties of divinity, medicine, law and engineering and as early as 1847 Cox was dreaming of a "great central University". Unfortunately in all his schemes he was dependant upon the financial support of Doctor Warneford, Rector of Bourton-on-the-Water, whose beneficence was accompanied by fears of "the subtle designs of the Jesuits and the insidious intrusion of malignant dissenters". These sentiments were out of tune with a town which was flourishing on the enterprise of dissenters, and allied with the

growing irascibility of Sands Cox they led to a period of growing debt and disorder in the affairs of Queen's College.

In 1882 the teaching of certain medical sciences was transferred from Queen's College to Mason College, and in 1892 the medical faculty of Queen's College became the Queen's Faculty of Medicine in Mason's Science College. The move was supported firmly, if sorrowfully, by all but one of the medical professoriate, and

250 medical students moved over to Mason College leaving behind them only 20 theological students. The local Press was withering in its criticism of Queen's College for "maundering on" with 20 students. "The College must be mended or ended" said the *Birmingham Gazette*. The building eventually closed but the name was revived in 1923 for the Church of England Theological College which now thrives in Somerset Road, Edgbaston.

ABOVE: The dissecting room of Queen's College, about 1880.

The bearded figure on the left is Charles Lapworth, Professor of Geology 1882-1913, whose world reputation still endures as the originator of the Ordovician System, a major division of geological time. He also identified the Moine Thrust, a major geological structure of North-West Europe, and demonstrated the value of the graptolite group of fossils in measuring the Earth's history. With him in this 1898 photograph are his assistant professor, W W Watts and (crouching) his demonstrator Frank Raw.

The picture far-left was taken on Saturday 30 May 1896 in Comley Quarry, Shropshire, where Lapworth identified the first Cambrian fossils in England and Wales. He conducted regular Saturday field trips to Shropshire, Aldridge and the lower Severn. This party took the train to Church Stretton and completed their journey on foot.

TOP RIGHT: W Hillhouse, Professor of Botany 1882-1909, was one of 12 professors and 50 others who in 1887 signed a document urging that a part of the Birmingham fund for celebrating the Queen's Jubilee should be devoted to founding a Midland university. He wrote of the proposal also in *The Midland Naturalist*, which he edited, but to no effect.

Hillhouse was also a leading advocate of university extension lectures, and after an earlier reverse he succeeded in persuading his colleagues at Mason College to adopt a scheme of "lectures and classes in populous places". Twelve years later this led to the University's close involvement with the Worker's Education Association—a name said to have been invented by Sir Oliver Lodge.

RIGHT: The bust of Dr Thomas Pretious Heslop subscribed for by the students of Mason College after his death in 1885. He gave 11,000 books to the College Library at a personal cost of more than £6,000 together with many complete sets of literary and scientific periodicals which were of especial value. His name is perpetuated in the present Heslop Room where rare books are housed.

The photographs on these four pages belong to a series taken by the London photographers Bedford Lemere in 1897 at Mason University College, as it had then become. BELOW: the Council Room with the half-length Munns portrait of Mason. RIGHT: A staircase. OPPOSITE: The Library and the Natural History Museum. Following pages, left to right: Physics Laboratory, Chemistry Laboratory, Aantomy Lecture Theatre, Anatomy Museum. The Anatomy and Medical Lecture Theatres were not in the original College plans but were built subsequently for the medical students of Queen's College. The Anatomy Theatre remained substantially unchanged until World War II when it was destroyed by a German fire-bomb.

The Hemsleigh Wedgwood Collection seen in the Library—mainly philological publications and dictionaries—was given in 1891.

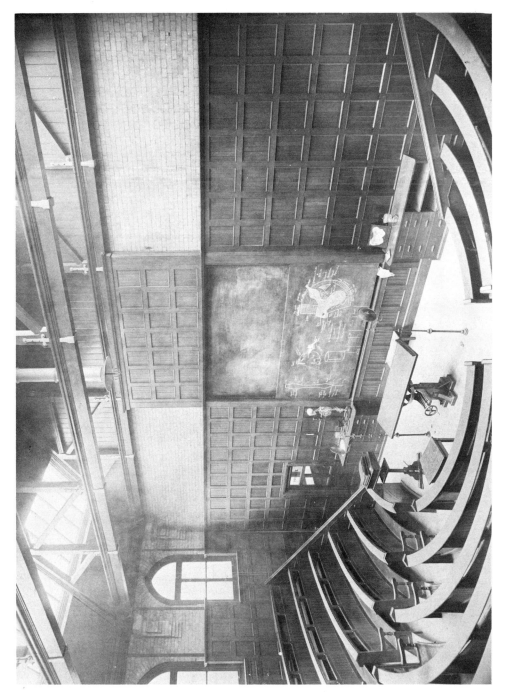

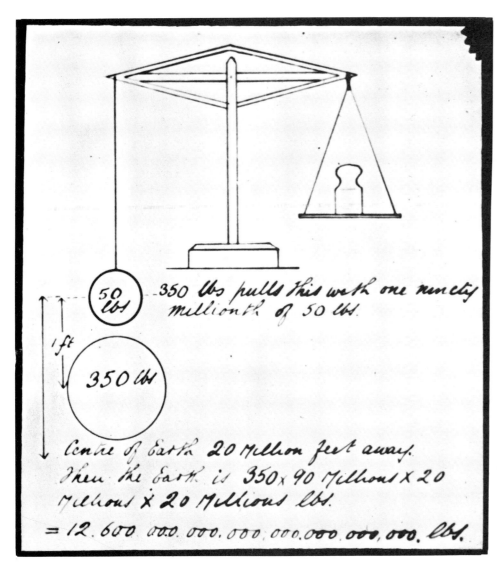

350 lbs pulls this with one ninety millionth of 50 lbs.

50 lbs

1 ft

350 lbs

Centre of Earth 20 Million feet away. Then the Earth is 350 × 90 Millions × 20 Millions × 20 Millions lbs.

= 12.600.000.000.000.000.000.000. lbs.

How to weigh the Earth. John Henry Poynting's ultra-simplified diagram of the famous experiment which in fact took him (with related experiments) twelve months to complete. The balance was made by Oertling of Germany in 1880 and is still used at the National Physical Laboratory, Teddington, for the accurate comparison of masses in the range 10 to 50 kilograms.

Poynting was Professor of Physics from 1880-1914, and Dean of the Faculty of Science from 1900 when the University was founded until his retirement. He set up the balance in a basement room of Mason College immediately below his own room. The windows were blocked up, a firm brick floor was layed, and in the pillars supporting the floor above he had rubber 'bricks' inserted. In the floor of his own room a circle about a yard wide was cut and a telescope was mounted there to observe the tilt of the beam. The hole, filled with concrete, could still be seen in 1960.

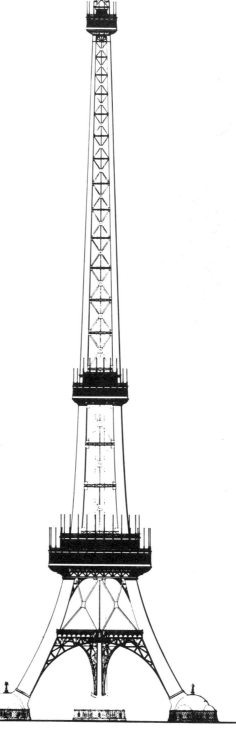

Robert Henry Smith became Professor of Engineering in the Imperial University of Japan at the age of 23, before coming to Mason College as its first Professor of Engineering. Like Eiffel in France he delighted in design exercises for tall buildings. The one on the left would have been 1400ft high—taller than the Eiffel Tower—had it been built, and notably different by virtue of its tripod base. The one below, well in advance of its time, was for an office tower block 500ft high with 31 floors and a central lift. Smith retired in 1896 to an extensive consulting practice in Westminster.

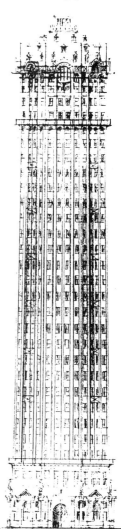

Sir William Tilden, first Professor of Chemistry in Mason College (1880-1894). He produced the first specimen of synthetic rubber from turpentine oil in 1892, in the course of research on terpenes (vegetable solutions which rotate the plane of polarised light). He also synthesised a new paraffin, carbon tetraethyl, and several coal tar derivatives. At the age of 80 he di...

y...... to a chair at the Royal College of Science, he returned to Birmingham in 1898 for for the crucial meetings which shaped the new University.

Edward Adolf Sonnenschein, Professor of Latin and Greek 1883-1918. He led a group of Arts professors nicknamed the *Boni* whose goal was a liberal, democratic and broad-based university. The late Sir Michael Sadler wrote: "His ..... into the fundamental princi..... lif..... .... resisted ....ight compromise academic liberty ..... At the critical moment Chamberlain concurred with Sonnenschein's convictions".

Son of a London schoolmaster, Sonnenschein took a first in classical moderations at Oxford followed by a first in litterae humaniores. He was an authority on Plautus and a distinguished grammarian, editor of the *Parallel Grammar* series. His *Soul of Grammar* was published only two years before his death at Bath, where he had retired.

Robert Samuel Heath, Principal of Mason College from the time the post was created in 1890, and Professor of Mathematics 1884-1918. He continued as Vice-Principal and Registrar ..e University under Sir Oliver Lodge ..1918 when he retired. The son of a ..lnshire farmer, he won a scholarship to ..n College where Tilden was one of his tutors. He graduated Second Wrangler at Cambridge and was a Fellow of Trinity before coming to Birmingham as Professor of Mathematics in 1884. Several of his students became first, second or third wranglers and achieved distinction in later life. His writings included *The dynamics of a rigid body in elliptic space* and *Treatise upon Geometrical Optics*.

Professor B C A (later Sir Bertram) Windle, first Dean of the Queen's Faculty of Medicine when it became a part of Mason College in 1892. There were no other deans at that time. He continued as Dean until 1905, when he became Principal of Cork University.

Windle was an able administrator who had played a leading part in the 1892 merger, and as President of the Birmingham Philosophical Society in that year he made his first of many statements in favour of a university. But his main objective was the power to confer degrees: medical students were being discouraged and at one stage reduced in numbers by the need to acquire qualifications from up to nine institutions elsewhere. He told Chamberlain that he thought £100,000 would be enough to get a charter and he revealed little sympathy with the broader concepts of Sonnenschein and Chamberlain.

Ever yours sincerely,
Constance C. W. Naden

The Mason College Union Committee of 1895-6, equivalent of the present day Guild of Students' Council. BACK: L Satchwell-Smith, Miss Fiedler, Miss Malins, Miss Ward, A H R Buller, A S Barnes. MIDDLE: T S Price, Miss Twigg, R H Pickard, Miss Suffield, Miss Lapworth. FRONT: G A Shakespear, F Jones.

Barnes is better remembered as Professor Stanley Barnes, Dean of the Faculty of Medicine (and, later, Dentistry) during the vital years 1930-41 when the new Medical School was being built and brought into use on the Queen Elizabeth Hospital site. In planning the new Hospital Centre he was closely helped by Professor W Billington who had been a fellow student at Mason College.

Buller was subsequently Professor of Botany in the University of Manitoba 1904-36.

Another of the group became Sir Robert Pickard, Director of the British Cotton Industries Research Association and former Principal of Battersea Polytechnic.

Gilbert Arden Shakespear joined Poynting's staff before 1900 and remained a lecturer in Physics until his retirement just before the Second World War; he married a fellow student who became Dame Ethel Shakespear, a distinguished palaeontologist, and they farmed together near Bromsgrove.

The professors' confidence in the quality of the education they provided is shown by the presence of Misses Fiedler, Malins and Lapworth.

ABOVE CENTRE: William Henry Austin, one of Heath's mathematics students, went on to Cambridge and was Senior Wrangler in 1897. He was a product of Jenkins Street Board School and KES Camp Hill. He returned in 1899 as a lecturer, but had his left leg amputated to check a sarcoma and died in 1902. A memorial fund was raised and now supports the W H Austin Prize in Pure Mathematics.

RIGHT: Constance Naden, philosopher and poet, whose death at 31 was commemorated by a marble bust and an annual medal (both still with us) and an effusive and elegantly bound memorial volume. To this Professors Lapworth and Tilden both contributed warm praise of both her friendship and her intellectual powers, having taught her after she enrolled at Mason College in 1881. Only Herbert Spencer, whose disciple she was, soured the tributes by observing that "mental powers so highly developed in a woman are in some measure abnormal, and involve a physiological cost which the feminine organisation will not bear without injury more or less profound". William Ewart Gladstone considered her poetry good, which it certainly is—and in parts very amusing in a frank, modern, Audenesque way.

Impressions after interview with
J. Chamberlain – Aug. 8th 1899.

1. It is not impossible that we may get what we want, *or part of it*, if we proceed by way of approaching the Charter Sub. Committee and the Professoriate in October. It is true that we cannot expect Mr. C. to assist us in getting our views brought forward in B'ham but if we can get the Professoriate and the Sub. C. to give us a fair hearing I think it will probably be within C's power to get the Charter modified in accordance with such views as may be then... powerfully backed, though I have no warrant *of present* for

continued overleaf

Ernest Gold in 1901, later CB, DSO, FRS. Still very alert at 94, living in Hampstead Garden Suburb, he spoke with affection of his time at Mason College (1897-1900) under Professor Heath. Son of a farmer at Rowington, Warwickshire, he went to Coleshill Grammar School, then Mason College, then Cambridge with the help of £50 borrowed from an insurance company. Third Wrangler in 1903 and a Fellow of St John's. For 41 years he served the Meteorological Office, retiring in 1947 as Deputy Director. The Americans gave him the Medal of Freedom with Silver Palm "for exceptionally meritorious achievement . . . . . His aggressive work, tireless efforts and close co-operation contributed in no small degree to the great success of the combined air operations." In 1908 he discovered the reason for the isothermal condition of the stratosphere, later putting it into light-hearted verse.

Charles Talbut Onions (1873-1965) from a portrait by William Dring RA in Magdalen College, Oxford. He became a principal editor of the Oxford Dictionary (*New English Dictionary on Historical Principles*) and *the* editor of the 'Shorter Oxford'. Educated at King Edward's Camp Hill and Mason College, he took a London BA in 1892 and an MA in Classics 1895. He then gave up his teaching job to join the Oxford Dictionary team, eventually becoming Reader in English Philology at Oxford 1927-49. He took over the Shorter Oxford in 1922 when two-thirds remained to be done and completed it for publication in 1933. The University of Birmingham gave him an honorary LLD in 1930.

Frederick John Marrian Stratton, DSO, OBE, TD, FRS (1881-1960). He became Professor of Astrophysics at Cambridge and Director of the Solar Physics Observatory. Son of *The Birmingham Post* music critic, he entered Mason College in 1897 to become another of Heath's mathematical prodigies, graduating Third Wrangler in 1904. From the appearance of Nova Geminorum in 1912 his special academic interest was in novae; but he was a man of many other interests. He served as Lieutenant Colonel with Signals in two world wars, and subsequently as an adviser to the Army Council. In peace he was a pillar of the British Legion. He shared with Sir Oliver Lodge an interest in psychical research, and was a devoted Unitarian, his parents having been members of the Church of the Messiah in Birmingham. The generals knew him as 'Don' and the dons as 'Chubby'. From 1901 Gonville and Caius College was his home.

Sonnenschein's draft record (in green ink) of the conversation in which he was assured of Chamberlain's support—provided he did not present an open challenge to the Senate, which had already rejected his views twice. Following that defeat it was G H (later Sir George) Kenrick who gave Sonnenschein the tip that his ideas had been accepted by Chamberlain and incorporated in the draft Charter. It was the great Unitarian families of Birmingham

continued overleaf

...saying.

...thinking that this will be the case.
It would have to be done by C's influence at the Com'ee of the Privy Council, where he is practically omnipotent: and I think he would not hesitate to act if he felt that he had behind him an entente cordiale of the local opinion, whereas he would not feel justified in supporting our views if coming from only a small band of Professors.

Here, then, it appears to me lies our chance; such as it is. It must be remembered that there is an impression in B'ham that C. would rather like to see some of our points brought in, & this might predispose the Charter Sub-C. to consider them favorably, or to allow us to approach C. on the subject.

2. To present a petition signed by only a small number of Professors at the present time would be to court defeat; for we should drive both the Sub-C. & the rest of the Professoriate into an attitude of opposition, & should so expose the weakness of our following. C. said that he thought it very doubtful whether such a petition would be successful, and that he would not be justified in giving it his support, after the general agreement which was arrived at at the Exec. Com'ee on May 31st.

3. The general attitude taken up by C. is no doubt due to him that even if the Charter is not further amended, it will be sufficient for providing a basis by which...

The University may be started in direction; that, in fact, our amendments are not absolutely necessary to secure the ends which we have in view, & with which in general he sympathises. But he said he had no wish to control our action, and that if we thought our amendments of sufficient importance to be pressed by a petition, he would not stand in the way of our going ahead with it.

4. C. expressed surprise at the suggestion that the Univ. might drop some of the Professors of M.C. who "have borne the heat & burden of the day", and declare that he for one would oppose any such action; "the Professors of M.C." he said "have the same chance of being elected to the Univ. chairs as have of being selected for West B'ham — that is practical certainty"...

---

who carried through the liberal solution against the earlier, more conservative views of the professors in Science and Medicine. Sonnenschein later acknowledged that it could not have been done without Chamberlain; equally it would not have been done without Sonnenschein as chief propagandist.

His main points were: that the university should be responsible simultaneously for teaching, research and awarding degrees; that all including students should have a voice in its government; that professors should have security of tenure; that the sovereign rights of faculties should be recognised.

In a private letter twenty years later Sonnenschein wrote: "During the years 1898-1900 I was in close touch with Mr Joseph Chamberlain, and was indeed honoured with his confidence. The fact is there were parties in Birmingham pulling different ways, especially in regard to what some of us regarded as an essential of a proper University—academic freedom. Mr Chamberlain was our ally in this matter, though we had to keep this private. In January 1899 a small body of which I was Chairman, sent him a carefully drawn up list of suggestions, and to our joy he accepted them and worked along those lines."

College into University

The two years in which Joseph Chamberlain brought the University of Birmingham into being were perhaps the most strenuous, and the bitterest, of his political career. As Colonial Secretary he was deeply involved in the Boer War, whose beginnings he had tried to suppress; and despite his denials the Lloyd George Liberals hounded him constantly with the accusation that he was prolonging the war to reap the profits from the arms and ammunition which his brother Arthur was making at the Kynoch factory in Birmingham. He defeated his enemies in the khaki election of 1900, but the bitter taste remained: "It has been fought with the greatest malignity by the baser sort on the other side" he wrote to his wife. That he could at the same time give close attention to the University project was a testimony to his capacity for public affairs.

He apparently took no interest in Mason College until after Mason's death in 1881, when he became one of the five additional trustees appointed by Birmingham Town Council under the trust deed. Thereafter his membership was continuous (though his attendances were inevitably few, so that on one occasion his fellow trustees passed a vote of thanks to him for attending) until January 1898, when by the Act of Incorporation of Mason University College he became its first President.

That Act transferred control of the College from a small private trust to a representative governing body of 180, similar to the later University Court of Governors; it was this which put Chamberlain in a position to direct and control events. But the specific purpose of the Act—to enable Mason College to join the Federal Victoria University, which the medical professors saw as a cheap and easy way of obtaining degree-conferring powers —was already a dead letter. For in November 1896, before it had reached the Statute Book, Chamberlain was asked by the Trustees to hear their and Senate's views on a Midland university, and the minutes describe his response thus: "Mr Chamberlain said that he looked forward to the establishment of a Midland University in Birmingham. He should object to any proposal for Mason College to become a constituent part of the Victoria University, or to the University being established without adequate funds. He hoped the Trustees would defer moving in the matter for a year or two in order that the appeal on behalf of the General Hospital might be out of the way. He thought that Nottingham and Bristol should be informed of the intention of Mason College to apply for an Act conferring University powers in about two years from the present time."

Within a month Senate had trimmed its sails to the Chamberlain wind. A report signed by Professors Heath (Principal), Windle, Barling, Poynting and T W Bridge—the Arts professors were unrepresented—accepted the concept of a new federal university centred on Birmingham, with direct encouragement of original research. But their attempt to regain the initiative was weakened by the following passage: "It is clear that a University of the Federal type cannot concern itself directly with the teaching of the Students in its Colleges. This part of the work must be left in the hands of the Colleges, each of which will, therefore, in its own district act in this respect as the University." Whatever the earlier thoughts of Chamberlain and his unofficial adviser Sonnenschein may have been—and certainly the latter had envisaged a Birmingham-Bristol-Nottingham federation in his *A Teaching University of the Midlands*—they quickly set their minds against what would be a university in name only, without funds, powers or teaching responsibilities.

Then Chamberlain visited Glasgow University, of which he had been elected Lord Rector, and came back filled with the idea that Birmingham must have its own University—liberal, broad-based, self-contained, complete. "If it is not the University of Birmingham I am out of it," he told the old Trustees, only a month before they became part of the new Court of Governors with Chamberlain as President.

Thereafter Chamberlain forced the pace. The Lord Mayor of Birmingham, Charles Gabriel Beale, gave a lunch for the new Governors and opened with a regressive view which he was never to repeat in his many years of devoted service as the University's first Vice-Chancellor: "We are not here to bury an obsolete trust . . . but to carry out absolutely the original intentions of the Founder." Chamberlain ignored this, and in the course of a major speech defined what he meant by a university: "A school of universal instruction, not confined to any particular branch of knowledge but taking all knowledge in its province. A place in which those who come to teach shall continue to learn and in which the work, the most important work, of original research shall be continuously carried on under favourable circumstances." It must be self-governing and independent, and have the power to confer degrees. He asked for £250,000 to endow 15 additional professorial chairs.

He made another speech after lunch to the Governors, and a resolution moved by Lord Windsor and seconded by Professor Tilden that they should seek a Royal Charter was carried unanimously.

The skirmishing over the constitution of the University was not over. Professor Windle still protested that "a large endowment is secondary to the obtaining of university powers" and "the course of teaching and study should be moulded by the Governing Body." But Chamberlain was now on his own ground where he could not lose: the issue had passed from the private to the public sector, and he alone had the ear of the Privy Council upon whom the final decision would rest.

The appeal was launched with £95,000 already promised, and Chamberlain himself brought back the fullest begging bowl. Lord Strathcona, the poor Scots boy who became the last Resident Governor of the Hudson's Bay Company, promised him £25,000 and later raised it to £50,000; Andrew Carnegie, the Scots-born Pittsburgh steel millionaire, did the same, and it is fairly clear that one was played off against the other. Sir Charles Holcroft, the Black Country mine owner and steelmaster, gave a first £25,000 which grew to £100,000. And it was to Chamberlain that Lord Calthorpe offered twenty-five acres of his Edgbaston estate, the first of several such gifts on which the University now stands.

The Royal Charter for the University was received in May 1900, and by the end of that year the appeal had raised £382,000.

9th May 1899

Dear Mr Chamberlain;

You have interested me in your proposed University at Birmingham for the People of the Midlands.

May I suggest that an opportunity exists for such an institution to perform a great Service upon the whole country.

After the members of the Iron & Steel Institute. had returned to New York from their tour of observation through the United States the officials dined with me. Many pleasing short speeches were made; the close of one I have never forgotten. A partner in one of your foremost Steel Companies said: "Mr Carnegie, it is not your wonderful machinery, not even your unequalled supplies of minerals, which we have most cause to envy. It is something worth both of these combined, the class of scientific young experts you have to manage every department of your works. We have no corresponding class in England.

Beginning of the letter in which Andrew Carnegie formally promised 'the last £50,000' of the £250,000 for which Chamberlain was appealing. To get the letter Chamberlain had to accept an invitation to lunch with Carnegie in his suite at the Langham Hotel ("Even Colonial Secretaries must find time to lunch") but the result was to double Carnegie's first offer made a month earlier.

In an earlier letter to John Morley Carnegie had described Chamberlain as "a dangerous demagogue . . . the wrecker of harmony wherever he goes." Later he sought his friendship, and paid him the final compliment of marrying his widow.

RIGHT: Chamberlain in soft collar and tweeds —taken at Highbury, his Birmingham home, in about 1885 by Thomas Lewis.

Copy — April 19.
Hane Wells
Great Shelford
Cambridge

Dear Lodge
I fancy this is intended for you to read but keep private to yourself — So I send it you.
Joe has a way of keeping his word
& yours
M Foster

2, GROVE PARK, LIVERPOOL.

(Chandler)

Copy — Highbury
Moor Green
Birmingham
Apl 17 1900

Dear Sir
I am desired by Mr Chamberlain to thank you for your letter of the 13th & "enclosure & to say that he is unable to write as he is laid up with influenza but that he would like to talk to you when he sees you in the House of Commons. Meanwhile I am to say that he thinks that Professor Lodge would do very well if he were willing to make the

Sir Oliver Lodge, Professor of Physics at Liverpool, at first declined the Principalship of the new University. This persuasive letter was written by Chamberlain's secretary to Sir Michael Foster, Professor of Physiology at Cambridge and MP for London University, who passed on a copy to Lodge, who made this copy. Lodge was evidently concerned lest his research might suffer for another part of the letter read: "This is Mr Chamberlain's only doubt. If he were certain that Professor Lodge would make some sacrifice for the sake of the Institution which has to be created Mr Chamberlain feels that in the long run he would have not a bad opportunity for research also." In the event Lodge brought his laboratory and assistants to Birmingham.

Lodge was born at Penkhull (Staffs) and educated at Newport (Salop) Grammar School. Events proved him to be a brilliant choice, though not the first one. Sonnenschein, who still enjoyed Chamberlain's confidence, had supplied a list of possible names in February 1900, and in May he was told in a private letter: "Mr Chamberlain has had an immense amount of trouble in endeavouring to find the right man, and has had several refusals including Professor Butcher of Edinburgh. But although it is impossible to find anyone who is absolutely ideal, it seems to Mr Chamberlain that Professor Oliver Lodge will fulfil almost all our requirements."

Lodge had demonstrated the first practical application of electromagnetic radiation to communication in 1894, though it was left to Marconi to develop it as radio. His love of the arts did much to heal the rift between the faculties. He and his wife entertained brilliantly at their big house *Mariemont*—former home of the Albrights, whose daughter Mary Deborah had married the Secretary of State for Scotland after leaving Mason College—and members of staff were regularly invited to meet such figures as Bergson, Bernard Shaw and William James.

Vanity Fair cartoons of Lodge (RIGHT) and Sir Charles Holcroft (ABOVE) who gave £100,000 to the University—half of it anonymously, including £25,000 earmarked for the clock tower.

5.

... you will think with one that it is letter I should not depart from this rule in ... case.

My ... will be forthcoming at any time, but it is not ... now as I should much prefer ... you one for the round sum of £50,000, when £250,000 have been procured from other

6.

53, CADOGAN SQUARE, S.W.

Sources. I however the Committee would prefer to have the cheque for the smaller sum at once I shall gladly send it.

Believe me to be my ... yours

Strathcona

The letter to Chamberlain in which Lord Strathcona intimated, almost casually, that he would be doubling his promised contribution to "the round sum of £50,000". He also wrote: "I am very sensible of the kind way in which you refer to my own little effort" and hoped that the University, while affording scientific teaching would "not overlook what is of not less importance—giving to its young men a sound Commercial education." Chamberlain suggested setting up a Strathcona Trust to support a Faculty of Commerce, but the giver was adamant that his name should not be revealed—even to Council. Sixty-five years later however his generosity was remembered in the naming of the Strathcona Building.

The Faculty of Commerce, the first such in Britain, was established in 1902 under the brilliant leadership of Professor Sir William Ashley, now also commemorated by the neighbouring Ashley Building.

RIGHT: Sir Oliver Lodge—a Whitlock (Birmingham) portrait.
FAR RIGHT: Charles Gabriel Beale, four times Lord Mayor of Birmingham, Vice-Chancellor (then a lay office) 1900-1912. His son Edmund Phipson was University Treasurer for nine years before becoming Pro-Chancellor 1939-47, and his grandson Charles is the present Treasurer. A Birmingham solicitor, he gave unsparingly of his time and money to the University. He lived at *Maple Bank*, a large house near the campus now scheduled as a site for student residence, and there entertained the British Universities Students' Congress from which grew the National Union of Students. He gave the students their first club in Edmund Street in 1905, and his wife—a Kenrick—was president of the committee which set up the first hall of residence, University House.

The University Council and Academic Staff in 1901

1 W T Madin (Dental Surgery)
2 Dr R C Farmer (Chemistry)
3 Godfrey Melland (Metallurgy)
4, 5 Day Training College staff
6 Dr C E Purslow (Midwifery)
7 Walter E Collinge (Zoology)
8, 9 not identified
10 Dr W R Innes (Chemistry)
11 George E Allen (Physics)
12 Dr C Leedham-Green (Bacteriology)
13 Frank Raw (Geology)
14 Anne Hollingworth Joyce (Headmistress Day Training College)
15 Florence C M Clark (Asst Mistress)
16 Annie E Warmington (Asst Mistress)
17 J D Whittles (Dental Histology)
18 not identified
19 W F Haslam (Anatomy)
20 J Coole Kneale (Materia Medica)
21 G A Shakespear (Physics)

22 not identified
23 Prof J T J Morrison (Forensic Medicine)
24 Prof J W Taylor (Gynaecology)
25 Prof E W Wace Carlier (Physiology)
26 Asst Prof W W Watts (Geology)
27 Prof W Macneile Dixon (English)
28 Dr John Humphreys (Dental Anatomy)
29 A E Donagan (Dental Mechanics)
30 Prof E B Whitcombe (Mental Diseases)
31 not identified
32 Prof R Saundby (Medicine)
33 Prof A Foxwell (Therapeutics)
34 Prof R F C Leith (Pathology)
35 R A Lyster (Forensic Medicine)
36 Prof Bennett May (Surgery)
37 Prof C Bevenot (French)
38 Prof T W Bridge (Zoology)
39 Prof Gilbert Barling (Surgery)
40 Prof Percy F Frankland (Chemistry)
41 Prof Edward Malins (Midwifery)

42 not identified
43 F R Greenwood (Materia Medica)
44 Alderman J H Lloyd (Council)
45 Prof J H Muirhead (Philosophy)
46 Neville Chamberlain (Council)
47 Prof W Hillhouse (Botany)
48 G W Grosvenor (Council)
49 Prof F W Burstall (Engineering)
50 Prof Adrian J Brown (Brewing)
51 C J Lewis
52 George H Morley (University Secretary)
53 Prof H G Fiedler (German)
54 Prof Charles Lapworth (Geology)
55 Dr W Wright (Anatomy—first Esquire Bedell)
56 Sir James Smith (Council)
57 Prof Priestley Smith (Ophthalmology)
58 G S Albright (Life Governor)
59 Alan Reynolds (possibly Alfred J Reynolds, rep. of City of B'ham on Council)

60 G J Johnson (Council—the original Mason College trustee)
61 Laurence W Hodson (Council)
62 Edwin Rickards (Council)
63 Hume C Pinsent (Council)
64 R F Martineau (Council)
65 Maurice Pollock (Council)
66 Prof B C A Windle (Anatomy—Dean of Medicine)
67 Prof R S Heath (Vice-Principal, Registrar and Mason Professor of Mathematics)
68 Dr Oliver J Lodge (Principal)
69 Samuel Edwards (Lord Mayor)
70 Joseph Chamberlain (Chancellor)
71 Ald C G Beale (Vice-Chancellor)
72 Francis Corder Clayton (Pro-Vice-Chancellor and Treasurer)
73 Prof J H Poynting (Physics—Dean of Science)
74 Prof E A Sonnenschein (Greek and Latin—Dean of Arts)

LEFT: Start of the first Degree Day procession on Saturday 6 July 1901. Dr W Wright, Esquire Bedell, leads with a borrowed mace; the University mace was a gift from Mrs C G Beale two years later. Behind him come the staff, proceeding from Mason College to the Town Hall.

ABOVE: The latter end of the procession with Joseph Chamberlain in the distance. The first eight (left to right as seen) are Professor P Smith, Sir James Smith, Charles Showell, A J Reynolds, Edwin Rickards, Maurice Pollock, Hume Pinsent, Alderman Martineau.

NEXT PAGE: The Chancellor, Joseph Chamberlain and Lord Mayor, Samuel Edwards.

The ceremony began at noon, but for an hour before 400 students (the medics carrying bottles and bones) passed the time with noisy songs—among them *Corpus Brovinum sub terra jacet sed anima vivet.*

The graduands were members of staff and Mason College students. The first Degree was conferred on the Principal, Sir Oliver Lodge, with the now time-honoured phrase: "By virtue of my authority as Chancellor, I admit you to the degree of Master of Science". The "totally new" degree of Master of Dental Surgery was incidentally conferred on John Humphreys, whose son was Vice-Chancellor half a century later.

The students had a song or a quip for everyone—*Beer, beer, glorious beer* for the brewing professor, Adrian Brown, and "Atishoo" for H W Pepper, MB chB. When the first lady was presented they shouted "Go on, Sir, kiss her". Chamberlain did not oblige. They bore him no grudge but sang *Good Old Joe* and *For He's a Jolly Good Fellow*, and when in appealing for funds he asked "What is half a million?" they thundered back as with a single voice "Nothing!"

33

The Executive Committee of the Students' Representative Council 1901/2. The University magazine named them as: back row, Mr Gebhard (Secretary), Miss Hilda Clark (Secretary), Mr Sargent (Vice-President), Mr Bowater, Miss Hawkes; front row, Miss Southall, Mr Barling (President), Mr Scott, Miss Ashford.

Norman Leslie Gebhard went on to get an MSc in Metallurgy in 1903 and later a PhD at Basle. After a short period as lecturer at Derby Technical College he became assistant manager of the Neva Stearme Works in Moscow 1908-14, and subsequently general manager of South African Oil and Fat Industries in Natal.

Margaret Mellard Hawkes is seen again (RIGHT) in her degree day photograph. She stayed to get an MA in 1902. From 1912 to 1919 she was doing private teaching at her home in Frederick Road, Edgbaston, and then became English mistress at Edgbaston College until 1924.

Another of the group is well remembered as Colonel William Bowater, MC, TD, MRCS, LRCP, BDS. He practiced in Birmingham as a dental surgeon, both privately and at the dental hospital, and saw active service in two world wars. His many interests included entomology and he produced a hybrid moth which bears his name. He was the son of Alderman Sir William Bowater, also a dental surgeon, who was five times Lord Mayor of Birmingham, a Governor of the University and President of the Dental Hospital.

The final year chemistry class of about 1904 with Professor Percy Faraday Frankland (centre, seated) and staff. Frankland held the Mason chair of chemistry from 1894–1918. He was the son of another famous chemist, Sir Edward Frankland, and got his middle name from his godfather, Michael Faraday.

Although his major research was in the field of stereochemistry, he also did a good deal of work on the bacteriology and purification of air and water. The precision of his experiments was a byword and other researchers corrected their results to conform with his. According to his obituarist "He was very insistent on scrupulous cleanliness and very critical of any untidiness. He was very stimulating when the work was well done. Carelessness of experiment, speech or thought made him very angry, sometimes violently so. He could not tolerate anything bogus or insincere".

He once appeared before the Birmingham Magistrates for trying to stop a policeman from arresting a small boy who had been picking up fallen apples; this did not prevent him from being appointed a J.P. himself, and he took the duty very seriously. During the First World War he was a member of the Admiralty Inventions Board and the Chemical Warfare Committee, and Deputy Inspector of high explosives for the Birmingham area. He was responsible for the adoption by Winston Churchill, then Minister of Munitions, of a method of preparing mustard gas which proved superior to that used by the Germans.

Francis William Aston (1877-1945), the first of three Nobel Prize winners in these pages. He was brought up at Tennal House, Harborne, where his father was a small farmer and metal merchant, and entered Mason College in 1893. Much of his early research was done in a loft at home. He later took a course in brewing and and worked for W Butler & Co of Wolverhampton. His first paper was published jointly with Frankland in 1901; his second appeared in 1905 in the *Proceedings of the Royal Society* by which time he had been inspired by the discovery of X-rays to concentrate on atomic physics. He had no degree until 1909 when the University gave him an official one on appointing him lecturer. After only one term he moved to the Cavendish Laboratory at Cambridge and entered Trinity College, his home for the next 35 years. There he demonstrated the isotopic nature of neon, chlorine and other elements and the whole numbers rule for atomic weight. His classic work

Isotopes was published in 1922, when he also received a Nobel Prize along with Bohr, Einstein and Soddy. Lord Rutherford was his close friend.

According to his obituarist: "To him as to so few, it was given to live in the way he most wanted. Whether designing or operating his mass-spectrograph, photographing the eclipse, gliding down the Alps on his skis, trying to hit the bull's eye in deck games or handling money affairs, fate almost invariably favoured him."

TOP CENTRE: Frank Percy Wilson (1889-1963) became Merton Professor of English Literature in the University of Oxford from 1947-57 and is still well remembered as a friendly visitor to the Shakespeare Institute. He came to the University from King Edward's School graduating BA 1911, MA 1912. He returned for two years as a lecturer after the First World War and took his DLitt in 1921. The University honoured him with an LLD in 1947.

TOP RIGHT: Sir Edward Elgar, first Professor of Music (1905-08). His appointment was a condition of the £10,000 given by Richard Peyton—a leading Birmingham Unitarian, with interests in the Midland Bank and the London Midland and Scottish Railway—to endow the Chair. Elgar's main duties were public lectures whose preparation (and reception) increasingly troubled him. *Mermaid* commented after his first lecture: "It can hardly be said that our new professor is a born speaker". He resigned after three years. His friend and successor, Sir Granville Bantock (RIGHT) held the Chair with great distinction for 26 years while continuing as Principal of the Birmingham School of Music. On his retirement in 1934 the Barber Trust provided sufficient money to make the Chair a full-time one.

Dental students of 1907. BACK, l to r; G D Ross-Watt, T P Brown, H F Humphreys, G K Wild, Miss Edwards, A T Knight, T N Jeffries, C W Nicholas, R Hodson. MIDDLE: S Shovelton, L G Jordan, Miss Hopkins, C Retallack, Mrs Wakefield (caretaker's wife), Trevor Matthews, G H Mackenzie. FRONT: A H Strong, W R W Booth, W F Birrell, F Thompson.

The photograph was taken at the old (then the "new") Dental Hospital in Great Charles Street. The Filling Room in 1901 (OPPOSITE) was at the earlier one in Newhall Street.

Humphrey Humphreys, distinctive in his Norfolk tweeds, later officiated as Student President at the opening of the Aston Webb buildings by Edward VII. In 1935 he became first Professor of Dental Surgery and in 1952-53 he was Vice-Chancellor and Principal of the University.

His father John Humphreys had been Professor of Dental Anatomy in Queen's College back in 1886, but it was 49 years before the University was to create a Chair of Dentistry, and he remained a lecturer until his retirement in 1919. He had a wide knowledge of natural history and archaeology, and was a welcome member of the History Students' Fellowship. The Odontological Museum and Chair of Dental Health bear his name.

The School had started at Queen's College in 1880, when the Dental Hospital was recognised by the Royal College of Surgeons. It has remained physically separate from the University in the centre of the City, but staff and students have probably contributed more than a proportionate share to the corporate life of the University.

These cartoons by Denis Gascoigne Lillie were published in the student magazine *The Mermaid* during 1904-6. None of the originals can be traced; Lillie is said to have given them away indiscriminately. Four later ones which he did at Cambridge are now in America, and another four are in the Scott Institute for Polar Research; of the earlier ones he did as a schoolboy at the United Services College, Westward Ho, there is no trace.

Lillie came to Birmingham University in 1903 to study Physics, Chemistry, Botany and Zoology and matriculated Class I in all subjects. But he failed all subjects in his first year and left in 1906 for St. John's College, Cambridge—where he graduated in 1909 and received his MA in 1914. A farewell note in *The Mermaid* said "we extend our most cordial thanks to Mr D G Lillie, who has graced our pages with his exceptional art, and wish him all success at Cambridge".

Probably he was one of those in the Medical Lecture Theatre on Saturday 17 December 1904 who gave Captain R F Scott (father of the present Chancellor) "one of the most vociferous welcomes he has received since his return from the Antarctic Continent". Lillie joined Scott's next and last expedition as Biologist in Charge on board the Terra Nova. The editor of the Natural History Reports wrote: "to his skill and energy the large and valuable marine collections are mainly due."

Apsley Cherry-Garrard in *The Worst Journey in the World* described him thus: "As Lillie squatted on the poop surrounded by an inner ring of jars and tangled masses of the catch, and an outer ring of curious scientists, pseudo-scientists and seamen, no find pleased him so much as the frequent discovery of Cephalodiscus Rarus. Its ancestor was a link between the vertebrates and the invertebrates."

In 1919 he suffered a mental breakdown from which he never recovered, and died in 1963 at Redhills Hospital, Exeter.

His Cambridge sketches included Sir Sidney Harmer, later Director of the Natural History Museum, South Kensington, and Sir William Ridgeway; they had belonged to Sir Arthur Shipley, Master of Christ's College, and passed to his nephew G E Hutchinson of Yale University. The four at the Scott Institute represent members of the *Terra Nova* expedition—G C Simpson, E A Wilson, T G Taylor and W M Bruce.

Clovis Bévenot, Professor of French 1889-1909. Inspired to come to England by reading Professor Max Müller on *The Science of Language*. Gained exhibition in Italian at Oxford, studied Sanskrit at Gottingen and contributed a Spanish grammar to Sonnenschein's Parallel Grammar series.

Professor Henry Poynting weighing the Earth; the two nurses are members of his staff, Dr G A Shakespear and Dr A de P Denning. This would have appealed to Poynting, who loved students and teaching. He won the Adams Prize in 1891 for his paper *The Mean Density of the Earth* and the Gold Medal of The Royal Society in 1905 for research on radiation.

A plumper Thomas Turner (first Professor of Metallurgy, 1902-26) than any of his photographs suggest. He had attended the Midland Institute and the Royal School of Mines before returning to Birmingham as a demonstrator in chemistry, later becoming a lecturer in metallurgy. He was also for eight years Director of Technical Education, Staffordshire. He is commemorated by the Turner Medal, the inscription on which reads that "his researches laid the foundation of scientific ironfounding". His son was Thomas Henry Turner (see later). Neville Chamberlain, Earl Baldwin and Sir Henry Fowler, (Director of Munitions Production, World War I) were among his Mason College pupils.

The academic status accorded to the new School of Brewing in 1899 evoked many popular gibes—to which its first Professor, Adrian J Brown (ABOVE) effectively replied by his analytical work during the arsenic poisoning scare of 1904 and by his subsequent election as FRS for research on enzymes. Educated at Burton-on-Trent Grammar School and the Royal School of Mines, he was a chemist with Salt's Brewery before coming to Birmingham.

Sonnenschein (see previously) was frequently cartooned with a tennis racket, as here.

Sir Oliver Lodge, on the other hand, was portrayed with a golf club, indicating that his Saturday afternoon journeys by train to Sutton Coldfield had not gone unobserved.

Gisbert Kapp, who at the age of 53 became the University's first Professor of Electrical Engineering (1905-19) at £1000 a year—reduced to £600 during the War at his own suggestion. He was already an electric power consultant of world repute, author of innumerable papers and patents, designer of Bristol's "Central Electric Lighting Station".

Born an Austrian, he had a Scottish grandmother and became a naturalised Briton in 1881. Another famous electrical engineer, S P Thompson FRS, got him to Birmingham by writing: "Birmingham University is going to appoint a Professor of Electrical Engineering at £1000 a year with freedom to practise professionally. Thou art the man—at least in my judgment. I am writing tonight to Sir Oliver Lodge to tell him so."

During his subsequent presidency of the Institution of Electrical Engineers Kapp was in hot water through criticising British industries for their backwardness in the use of electric power; typically, he stuck to his guns.

In 1905 the Guild of Undergraduates invited the Lord Chancellor, author of *Halsbury's Laws*, to be their Warden. Their own Chancellor's sharp reaction (ABOVE) did not blind him to the publicity value. The Warden delivered his address at the Midland Institute two days after this letter was written, making the criticism that the University had "a professor neither of Latin nor of Greek"—Sonnenschein being Professor of both. Afterwards Chamberlain took the party to the new buildings at Edgbaston.
LEFT TO RIGHT, SEATED:
Sir Oliver Lodge, Lord Halsbury, Joseph Chamberlain, Lord Avebury. STANDING: Austen Chamberlain, R B Haldane, Lord Milner.

Avebury was a wealthy banker with extensive academic pursuits and author *inter alia* of *The Pleasures of Life* which sold 259,000 copies. Austen Chamberlain, Joseph's son, was Chancellor of the Exchequer; his knighthood came later. Haldane was Secretary of State for War, subsequently becoming Lord Chancellor. Milner had been Governor of the Cape of Good Hope during the Boer War and became Secretary of State for War 1918-19.

The students had evidently had the Chancellor's observations passed on to them, but were no whit abashed. In the next issue of *The Mermaid* they observed: "A number of the authorities appear to be rather surprised that so

busy and important a personage should have consented to occupy the position—surprised that we should have had the audacity even to ask him—and still more surprised that the members of the committee should have had the ability to successfully organise so important a meeting as that held on May 13th, when Lord Halsbury addressed us. For ourselves, neither of these facts appears at all remarkable".

They added (agreeing with Chamberlain) that "the Arts side being, although an important, still only a secondary part of our college, the arrangement of having a combined chair of Latin and Greek is quite sufficient for our present needs".

The Siemens' patent steel smelting furnace (LEFT) was first brought into use in 1904 in the metallurgical laboratories, which stood alongside the old power station on the site now occupied by Mechanical Engineering. The lecture rooms were in C Block of the Aston Webb Buildings, which like A and B blocks was complete and in use long before the Royal opening. An article in *Engineering* said: "This building is believed to be a more lofty, better lighted, and more complete and compact smelting laboratory than at present exists anywhere for metallurgical instruction, not even excepting the great American universities."
ABOVE: The original Foundry.

Gilbert Shaw Scott took the first MSc in Metallurgy (1907) and became the first Secretary of the Institute of Metals, which had its office inside the Metallurgy Department. He married the Professor's daughter, Christie Turner. He had an infectious enthusiasm for motoring even before 1900, and in later years had the rare honour of being elected a Vice-President of the AA. For more than 40 years he was motoring correspondent of *The Birmingham Post*. He was a tireless diarist all his life from his days at Queen Mary's Grammar School, Walsall. RIGHT: With his 2½hp Singer and two seater trailer outside his parents' home, Doveridge, Four Oaks. The photograph was taken about 1902, before there were such things as number plates.

LEFT: The Faculty of Commerce in 1907. Sir William Ashley (centre) was the first Professor of Commerce 1901-25, and Dean of the Faculty 1902-23. He was a poor London boy who made his way to Balliol by hard work and scholarships, becoming Professor of Economic History at Harvard. His great academic achievement was to turn economists from their preoccupation with ideal models to a study of the real world of industry and commerce. He descended from his Harvard pinnacle for the chance of putting his ideas into practice at Birmingham.

Of the City he came to his daughter Anne wrote: "A leading place was taken by a group of interrelated Unitarian families, Beales, Chamberlains, Kenricks, Nettlefolds. These had become the local aristocracy and showed a commendable sense of *noblesse oblige*, giving themselves freely to the work of administrating the Town, the University and various forms of social work".

On Ashley's left is Frank Tillyard, Lecturer in Commercial Law, and on his right A W Kirkaldy, Professor of Finance. Tillyard later held the Chair of Commercial Law 1914-30 and was knighted for his work in connection with courts of referees and wages councils. Indeed, the chairmanship of the Stamped or Pressed Metal Wages Council was held for the whole of its 55 years' existence, except for one short interruption, by members of the Faculty.

The Japanese connection evident in the photograph began when a member of the Mitsui family came to Birmingham to study— in defiance of his guardian's wishes, it was said. By 1923 he had become Baron Mitsui, controller of the mighty Japanese conglomerate of that name, and he gave £5,000 to establish the Mitsui Chair of Finance. The link endures; a Mitsui research post has recently been established in the Department of Economics.

3, YATELEY ROAD,
EDGBASTON.

June 24. 1905.

Dear Mr. Lloyd,

I am just now engaged in one of the most important parts of my task at the Univ.? viz. in finding business openings for the graduates of the Faculty of Commerce. The majority, I hope as a rule, will have openings provided for them by their families & friends; but there will always be some who have no family business backing. We do not encourage such lads to come to us unless they have more than usual ability; but where there is ability, we ought to receive such boys as student. It is desireable in the interest of the nation; it is desireable also in the interest of the Faculty of Commerce, for nothing keeps up the standard

the success of the first few graduates. And as I know you take a real interest in the work of the Faculty of Commerce, I feel sure you will give this matter your early & sympathetic attention.

Yours very truly
W. J. Ashley.

ABOVE: The first and last pages of an 8-page letter written by Sir William Ashley to J H Lloyd, member of the firm which is now Stewarts and Lloyds, who served the University as Pro-Vice-Chancellor and then Deputy Pro-Chancellor from 1921-39. Ashley was seeking a job for one of his students. He took great pains to describe at length the young man's training and ability and the ways in which he might be employed.

Apparently there was no vacancy at Lloyds but a similar letter led to the young man— Wilfred Bland, son of a Kidderminster draper— being placed with W & T Avery Ltd. He did well there and was sent to the United States where he subsequently set up his own business.

Margery Fry (in uncharacteristic finery, LEFT) was visited at Somerville College, Oxford, by Professor Muirhead's wife and persuaded to become the first Warden of University House, 1904-14. Her father was Sir Edward Fry—judge, diplomat, member of the Bristol cocoa family. Her career as Principal of Somerville, secretary of the Howard League for Penal Reform, Governor of the BBC, member of the University Grants Committee was still to come.

She endowed 'House', as it is still affectionately known, with an indefinable but unmistakeable *esprit de corps* which has survived the years. It was the first university hostel for women, the first to admit male guests (see the handwritten dance programme, RIGHT) and later the first to admit male residents. It began in an old house at 215 Hagley Road, of which a typical study-bedroom is shown right. The group photograph

was taken in the garden there with Margery Fry FRONT CENTRE; on her left is Rose Sidgwick, her Oxford friend, who came to Birmingham as a history lecturer in 1905 and stayed until 1918, when she died of influenza while on a British universities mission to USA.

Margery Fry found C G Beale "pompous and rich" on first acquaintance, but her maturer judgment was: "I had great luck in being taken by the hand by a man named Beale . . . . a great power, and in some ways a great man." He made her a member of Council and other committees, to which she added innumerable causes of her own—Staffordshire Education, King Edwards Foundation, school medical services, mental deficiency legislation and smelling drains. A doggerel ABC handed round the Staffordshire Education offices included—

F for Miss Fry whom none can aroint
Who always is talking, and ever with point.

When the present University House (see later) was built in 1908, with Neville Chamberlain as chief fund-raiser, she wrote to her friend F N Wedgwood at the Etruria Potteries for crockery at wholesale prices; his reply (FIRST PAGE, OPPOSITE) consented to supply her direct because "oddly enough" there was no shop in Birmingham retailing his wares—"all there are despicable and of none account". When an inventory was taken before handing over University House to the Army in 1914 it included 717 pieces of Wedgwood tableware, cream.

THJ

UNIVERSITY

HOUSE . . .

1914

1.	Valse	Miramar	A. Hazeldine
2.	Valse	O! O! Delphine	M. Tomlinson
3.	One-Step	On the Mississippi	Miss Laws
4.	Valse	Pink Lady	E. M. Pickering
5.	Valse	Girl on the Film	A. Jones
6.	One-Step	Snookey Ookums	Wright
7.	Valse	Dancing Mistress	M. Chataway
8.	Lancers	Ragtime Lancers	J. H. Moss (Kadest)
9.	Valse	Un Peu d'Amour	Miss Unstal
10.	Valse	Passing of Salome	N. Wright
11.	Valse	Smiles then Kisses	Miss Kadest
12.	Valse	Girl from Utah	W. Bovend
13.	One-Step	Hullo- Ragtime	L. Bone
14.	Valse	The Glad Eye	Miss Ellwood
15.	Valse	Marriage Market	Burns
16.	Valse	Where my Caravan has rested	La Fitt Stureley
17.	One-Step	Wedding Glide	Tomlinson
18.	Valse	Pearl Girl	S. Pella
19.	Valse	Verveine	D. Chataway
20.	Valse	Little Grey Home in the West.	Wood

ABBEY LANDS,
STAFFORD

28/6/08.

Dear Miss Fry.

As you say we are wholesale folk & therefore ought not to deal with friends direct but I think you are now ruled by an

Had we any retail Birmingham that was of

day the case would be but oddly enough there is

shop, all there, are

of real account

The large mining laboratory (GENERAL VIEW ABOVE, detail of plant for treatment of ores TOP RIGHT) on the ground floor of C Block at Edgbaston was in use by 1906. Nearby was the model coal mine, with its mile of galleries in which students learned underground surveying, ventilation and safety precautions; it is still used by local fire services for smoke practice, the entrance being a small red-brick building near the South Car Park. The sketch (RIGHT) was by William Gray, who graduated in 1913 and became a mining engineer in Northern Nigeria; he should not necessarily be blamed for the punning caption.

These facilities were planned and initiated by Sir Richard Redmayne, Professor of Mining 1902-08. He left to become Chief Inspector of Mines at the Home Office, and was succeeded by a 31-year old Inspector of Mines, Dr John Cadman, who stayed until 1922 when he was appointed Adviser to the Cabinet on coal and petroleum. He raised considerable sums to found a School of Oil Engineering, now the Department of Chemical Engineering, and subsequently became Sir John, later Lord Cadman.

By our Gray(t) Artist

Pomp & Circumstance

Sir Aston Webb was commissioned to design the new University buildings at Bournbrook in the last year but one of Queen Victoria's reign; the result was in tune with the imperial dignity which that fashionable architect bestowed earlier upon the Victoria and Albert Museum and (less imperially) Birmingham's Victoria Law Courts, and later upon the Royal College of Science and Admiralty Arch.

The ornate style was perhaps inevitable in its day; the scale was another matter. Many were critical, though few openly so, of the spending on new buildings—in particular, on the Chamberlain Tower. That they provided a valuable, and perhaps indespensable, foundation for the University's subsequent and continuing eminence in the applied sciences is clear in retrospect. It was less clear to those who had to run things on a shoestring in the years up to 1914.

Before Andrew Carnegie converted him to a belief in new buildings, Joseph Chamberlain had launched his first appeal with the argument that 15 new professorial chairs were needed. In the event, between 1900 and 1914 the number of professors increased by one only, to thirty-one.

In 1905 he announced that nearly half of the million pounds sought had been raised. That meant only £100,000 in the previous five years, and the going was to be even slower—particularly after a stroke in 1906 restricted his own fund-raising activity. A further appeal in 1908 for £250,000, in anticipation of the royal opening, raised only £78,000, of which £30,000 came from Sir Charles Holcroft.

But outside the public appeal other loyal friends continued their support, in vivo or posthumously: £12,000 from the family of Charles Harding to build the present Law Library; a second £20,000 in the will of John Feeney (of The Birmingham Post) for a Chair of Metallurgy; £18,000 from Sir George Kenrick for a Poynting Chair of Physics (adding to his previous £25,000); £14,000 from the Beale Memorial Fund for a chair of Civil Engineering, C G Beale having died in 1912; £20,000 in the will of Thomas Best. Earlier than all these, Sir James Chance had endowed a Chair of Mechanical Engineering with £50,000.

It was not by accident that so many gifts were tied to specific purposes, for Lloyd George had grudgingly raised the Exchequer grant to £15,000 only on condition that any new 'free' money should be used to reduce the debt, which by 1913 was £160,000. He had also criticised the poor level of local support, as a result of which the City Council was persuaded to raise its contribution from ½d to a penny rate, later stabilised at £15,000 a year; this too had strings attached—fifteen free scholarships and more extramural classes.

The University was too poor even to afford a transmitter to attach to the aerial which Sir Oliver Lodge had strung from Mason College to the Norwich Union Building. Gloomily, he said in his last pre-war report: "Under the influence of the Chancellor buildings on a great scale were here provided; but to maintain corresponding staff and equipment has been a great burden all through my time of office".

However, these troubles were forgotten in the general euphoria when, on 7 July 1909, King Edward VII and his Queen came to open the new buildings of the University of Birmingham.

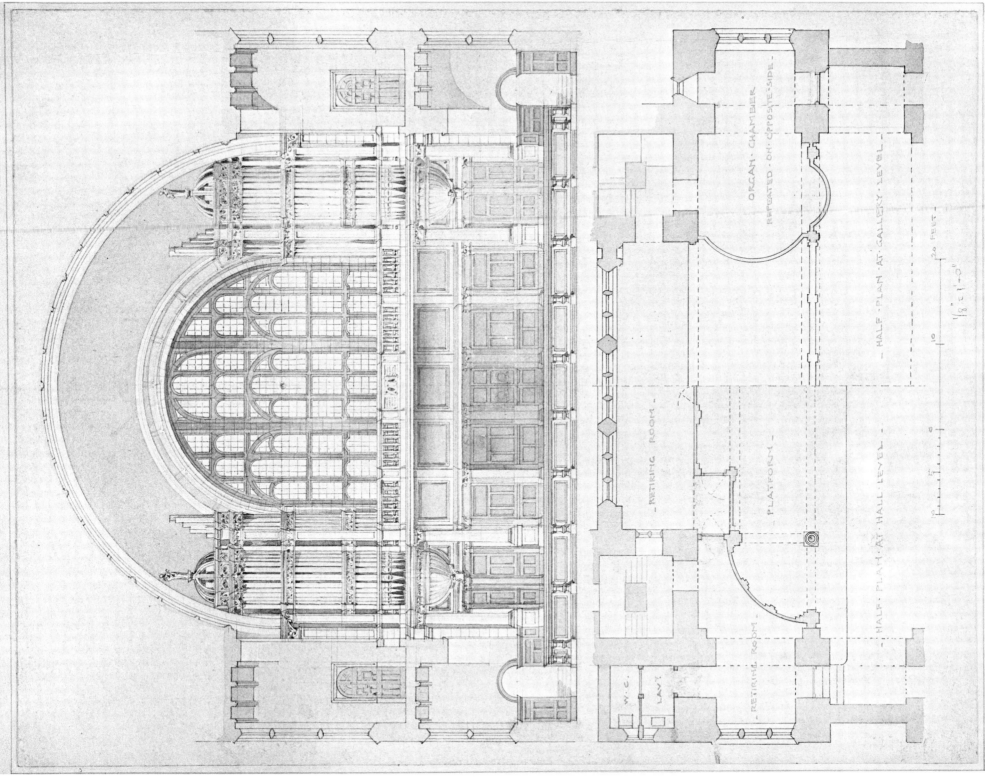

DRAWING Nº 340ᴮ

ORGAN · CHAMBER ·

REPEATED · ON · OPPOSITE · SIDE ·

· RETIRING · ROOM ·

· PLATFORM ·

· RETIRING · ROOM ·

W.C.

LAV.

· HALF · PLAN · AT · HALL · LEVEL ·

· HALF · PLAN · AT · GALLERY · LEVEL ·

⅛" = 1'-0"

20 FEET

· BIRMINGHAM : UNIVERSITY ·

· SECTION · THRO ' · HALL · LOOKING · SOUTH ·

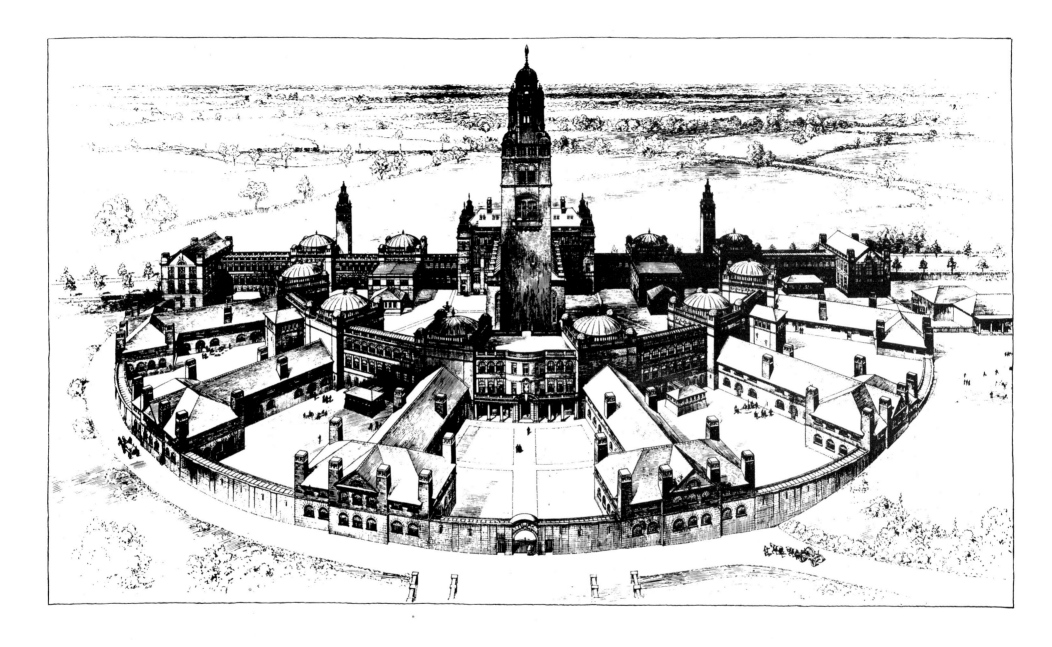

This first sketch for the Edgbaston buildings presents the concept of a semi-circular walled city that Sir Aston Webb retained throughout. In other respects there are marked differences from the final version.

Here six blocks radiate outward from the centre. The central tower is notably shorter than its successor, and different also in being in architectural harmony with the rest. The Great Hall lies dwarfed behind it instead of standing dominant on the periphery of the arc.

The two minor towers did not reappear in later designs, but the domes overlooking University Road—four in this sketch, later reduced to two—remained the architect's firm intention, though never implemented.

The later re-siting of the Great Hall at the periphery reduced the number of radial blocks from six to four, of which only three were in fact completed.

The single gateway on this side of the site was described as the Students' Entrance.

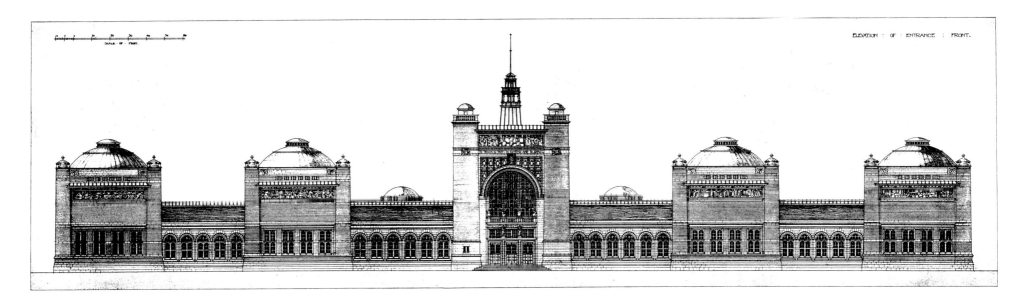

These sketches of 1902 brought the design nearer to final form. The height and style of the tower have changed little, but the Great Hall is now in its right place—though still without a dome, and without either the frieze over the main doors that appeared in a later sketch, or the individual figures in niches that replaced it. The two smaller domes belong to the entrance turrets behind the connecting blocks adjacent to the Great Hall; they were omitted from the final design. Note that the only windows in the front elevation are on the ground floor, and the height of the blocks at the rear is one storey less than in the final scheme.

54

BIRMINGHAM·VNIVERSITY
ELEVATION·TOWARDS·VNIVERSITY·ROAD

ELEVATION TOWARDS UNIVERSITY Rᴰ

Sɪʀ Aꜱᴛᴏɴ Wᴇʙʙ R·A & E·Iɴɢʀᴇꜱꜱ Bᴇʟʟ Aʀᴄʜᴛˢ

Final elevation from University Road. The tower is 'Big Joe' as we know it today, except that the clock face appears here at a lower level. The entrance gates with the Harding Library above them (CENTRE OF DRAWING) were completed in the first wave of building 1905-09, but stood in isolation for twenty years. The sections at the two extremities were also built in isolation, and later given their present names—Frankland Chemistry (RIGHT) and Poynting Physics. The gap between the Frankland and Harding buildings was closed in 1927 to provide accommodation for Biology and Brewing, now occupied mainly by Law; this new section followed closely Aston Webb's design, but omitted the dome over the centre portion, and in recent years the ground floor of this portion has been converted into an open passageway between Chancellor's Court and University Road.

The gap on the other side, reduced slightly by a short extension in modern style to Poynting Physics, is now officially permanent, and the end wall of the Harding Library has been finished off with a handsome bay window.

The affinity between the Harding-Frankland group and Poynting Physics is no longer apparent owing to the latter being partly obscured by new building.

The dome visible behind the clock tower belongs to the Great Hall, and the remaining four to the blocks linked with it. Of these, three were completed in the first building wave; the fourth (dome left of drawing) is no longer planned.

The quite different new Clock Tower, 325 ft high, was based closely on the Mangia Tower in Siena, which Joseph Chamberlain had greatly admired. It came into the plans at a late stage, and in a curious way.

On 1 October 1905 *The Birmingham Post* reported that Chamberlain had announced to the University Council "a little surprise"—an anonymous gift of £50,000. (The donor was, in fact, Sir Charles Holcroft).

Two months and seven days later the *Post* reported: "The anonymous gift which we announced last (*sic*) month was intended to include the erection of a tower in connection with the new buildings at Bournbrook, at a cost estimated by the architects at about £25,000. The tower, which it was suggested would be upwards of 300 ft in height, would not only form the main architectureal feature of the University but would be useful in connection with the Physics Department and as a record tower." No source was given for this addendum.

FAR LEFT: This sketch of the Great Hall entrance was exhibited at the Royal Academy Exhibition of 1907. Sir Aston Webb later became the first architect to be President of the Royal Academy since 1805.

LEFT: The tower in course of erection. It was built from the inside, without scaffolding, up to the level of the balcony. The base is solid concrete, 50 ft square by 10 ft thick, resting on bed rock 31 ft below ground. Thomas Rowbotham, main contractor for the other buildings, met the cost of clock and bells—and was especially praised for his generosity, having failed to win the contract for the tower. Joyce of Whitchurch built the clock, the face of which is 17ft 3in across; the largest bell weighs 6½ tons; the minute hand is 13ft 6ins long. There are ten floors served by an electric lift, but they are not on the University's official capacity record. In 1914 Physics strung a radio aerial across to the Harding Library, and in 1940 Sir Mark Oliphant used the tower for radar experiments. It has also supported a BBC relay dish.

Carved in stone round the tower are the words: THIS TOWER COMMEMORATES THE FOUNDING OF THE UNIVERSITY THROUGH THE INITIATIVE AND ACTIVE ENCOURAGEMENT OF ITS FIRST CHANCELLOR THE RIGHT HONOURABLE JOSEPH CHAMBERLAIN.

RIGHT: The steel framework of a dome under construction.

NEXT TWO PAGES: The front and rear of the Aston Webb complex with building still in progress. The uneven site, with a fall of 40 ft from front to rear, presented major problems, and from 1903-06 there were nearly 400 men continuously employed, fewer thereafter up to 1909. All the earth-moving was done by horse, cart and shovel. One night a spectacular fire destroyed the stables, but the horses were led to safety.

The power station (on the site now occupied by Mechanical Engineering) was the first building to be finished. From it a subway to the main buildings, 6 ft high and 10 ft below ground, carried gas, steam and waste water

pipes. Blocks A, B and C were built next— the first two for Electrical and Mechanical Engineering, the third for Mining and Metallurgy. Beneath the Great Hall were the dining hall, staff dining room and kitchens.

The original campus was small, being bounded on the north by University Road and on the south by a road almost adjacent to the

buildings. The area from here to the Bristol Road was used by the Birmingham Volunteers as a rifle range, but when they vacated it in 1907 Lord Calthorpe made it his second gift, of 20 acres, to the University. Until this was developed as playing fields the only sporting facilities were two tennis courts where the Haworth Chemistry building now stands, and a

bowling green for staff laid out and provided with a pavilion by George Cadbury.

LEFT: Bowed heads, feather boas and heavily trimmed hats mark the procession of King Edward VII, Queen Alexandra and the Princess Victoria through the Great Hall to perform the official opening. The date was 7 July 1909, chosen as a mark of royal esteem for Joseph Chamberlain, whose 73rd birthday it was. The effects of a severe stroke kept him confined to his home at Highgate, but his wife was there as Lady Mayoress.

The day had begun wet and cold when the royal party arrived at New Street Station, but the sun came out as their carriage was escorted by the silver-breasted Life Guards, with out-riders and trumpeters in scarlet and gold, to the Council House, where the Lord Mayor, Alderman G H Kenrick, was knighted. Extravagant arches spanned the streets —devised *inter alia* by the Fire Brigade, the Gas Department, the Water Department, the Cycle Trades and ("displaying brilliantly polished brass knobs") the Metallic Bedstead Manufacturers. Flags, shields, crowns, palms, shrubs and crimson carpets adorned the route. Muslin messages proclaimed in letters two feet high "King Edward the Peacemaker", "Prosper the University" and (somewhat irrelevantly) "Dieu et Mon Droit".

At the Council House the Queen wore dove grey crepe de chine and a small toque trimmed with grey feathers, Lady Lodge pale blue Ottoman silk and a tight bonnet edged with beads. The large reception room was re-furnished as the King's drawing room with Louis Quinze pieces and Persian carpets. Lunch began with *Tartelettes de Caviar* and ended with *Jambon de Yorc à la Gelée au Clicquot*, after which the party proceeded to Bournbrook through more streets lined with bunting and singing children. A 21-gun salute signalled the moment of the official opening, and the King's Superintendent of Police "whizzed past in his motor-car". Long after the royal party had left for home the fun continued in brightly lit streets made brighter by an illuminated tram-car.

"One painful note was introduced into the record" said the *Post*. A piece of falling masonry killed George Lemon, aged 50, patternmaker.

RIGHT: The Royal party leaving the Council House for Bournbrook.

LEFT: The opening ceremony on the platform of the Great Hall. ABOVE: this keyed photograph taken a moment or two later shows **1** The King **2** The Queen **3** Princess Victoria **4** The Recorder, J S Dugdale **5** The Town Clerk, E V Hiley **6** Miss Impey **7** The Pro-Vice-Chancellor, F C Clayton **8** The Bishop's Chaplain, Canon Hobhouse **9** Mrs Joseph Chamberlain, Lady Mayoress **10** Hilda Richards, the Chancellor's grand-daughter **11** The Bishop of Birmingham, Charles Gore **12** Lieut Gen Sir Charles Douglas **13** The Lord Mayor, Sir George Kenrick **16** Lord Knollys **24** Minister for War, R B Haldane **25** The Vice-Chancellor C G Beale **26** The Principal, Sir Oliver Lodge **27** Dean of Commerce, William Ashley **28** Vice-Principal, R S Heath **29** Dean of Medicine, Gilbert Barling **30** Contractor, Thomas Rowbotham **31** Dean of Arts, Alfred Hughes **32** Sir Aston Webb **33** Dean of Science, Henry Poynting **34** University Secretary, George H Morley **35** President of the Guild of Undergraduates, Humphrey F Humphreys **36** President of the Guild of Graduates, Dr A de P Denning.

RIGHT: The Water Department arch. Chamberlain had been a prime mover in piping Welsh water to Birmingham.

Highbury,
Moor Green,
Birmingham.

June 19/1909

My dear Principal

I am in receipt of your letter of the 15th inst. enclosing a list of the persons whom the Senate wishes to invite to accept the Honorary Degree of LL.D.

in other ways distinguished and that you should be careful as a University not to make it common, in which case I am afraid we shall have many refusals. As you know the Universities of Oxford & Cambridge as well as those of Dublin & Wales are freed in this particular, and I should not like to see our University taking a second place. I think the first

and instead, I would like to see inserted the names of:—

The Right Hon A. J. Balfour, Sir Charles Holcroft, & Lord Strathcona.

I think that the Honorary Degree ought to be kept for those exceptionally qualified or

---

With the royal opening less than a month away, Sir Oliver Lodge submitted to the Chancellor the Senate's list of nominations for the University's first honorary degrees, to be conferred later that year.

These extracts from Chamberlain's reply show that, although the stroke he had suffered during the celebration of Austen's wedding kept him from all public engagements, his mind remained alert and his interest keen.

But for his intervention two leading benefactors of the University, Sir Charles Holcroft and Lord Strathcona, would have gone unhonoured. He failed, however, in his objective of keeping the list short, for the outcome of this battle of wills was that *both* lists (the Senate's and his own) were retained, and 33 honorary degrees were conferred—far more than in any subsequent year.

One principle enunciated by Senate, but not subsequently maintained, was that preference should be given to those who had not previously been honoured by other universities. Chamberlain suggested that if this principle were considered important the list should omit himself, he having already received honorary degrees from Oxford, Cambridge, Dublin, Glasgow and Wales. Needless to say, his name remained.

The strict confidentiality that now attaches to honorary degree nominations was apparently not fully developed, for two years later the Prime Minister of New Zealand, Sir Joseph Ward, had the embarrassment of hearing Lodge announce that all the Commonwealth prime ministers except himself (they were in London for the coronation of George V) had declined the honour.

ALDERMAN G.H.KENRICK

LORD MAYOR

BIRMINGHAM UNIVERSITY OPENED JULY 7TH BY
THEIR MAJESTIES KING EDWARD VII & QUEEN ALEXANDRA.

Birmingham University

ALDERMAN C.G. BEALE

THE RIGHT HON. J. CHAMBERLAIN

SIR OLIVER LODGE

VICE CHANCELLOR OF THE UNIVERSITY

CHANCELLOR OF THE UNIVERSITY.

PRINCIPAL OF THE UNIVERSITY.

BIRMINGHAM UNIVERSITY OPENED JULY 7TH BY
THEIR MAJESTIES KING EDWARD VII & QUEEN ALEXANDRA.

It was the golden (or perhaps gilded) age of souvenirs, novelties, cheap trinkets and baubles of all kinds; modern wage and cost structures had not yet intervened in favour of the limited product range and the long manufacturing run. So the Royal visit was a bonanza not only for the Birmingham badge, medal and cutlery trades but also for potters and printers from far afield.

The postcards reproduced here are an interesting example of early colour printing. The bronze medal (obverse and reverse) hung from a replica of the University arms with a safety pin indicating that it was intended to be worn; it was one of many, in metals ranging from gilt to pewter. The ribbon plate bears no potter's mark.

TO COMMEMORATE THE OPENING OF THE BIRMINGHAM UNIVERSITY 1909

The professoriate in 1910.

BACK ROW: John Cadman (Mining), Karl Wichmann (German), Charles Raymond Beazley (History), E W Wace Carlier (Physiology), Frederick W Gamble (Zoology), Adrian J Brown (Brewing), A W Kirkcaldy (Finance), George S West (Botany).

MIDDLE: Granville Bantock (Music), Priestley Smith (Ophthalmology), unidentified, John Henry Muirhead (Philosophy), Jordan Lloyd (Surgery), Percy Frankland (Chemistry), R F C Leith (Pathology), Stephen M Dixon (Civil Engineering), J T J Morrison (Forensic Medicine).

FRONT: Edward Malins (Midwifery), Charles Lapworth (Geology), W J Ashley (Commerce —Dean of Faculty), J Henry Poynting (Physics —Dean of Science), Sir Oliver Lodge (Principal), R S Heath (Vice-Principal), Gilbert Barling (Surgery—Dean of Medicine), Alfred Hughes (Education—Dean of Arts), E A Sonnenschein (Latin and Greek), A Bostock Hill (Hygiene and Public Health).

The last named, who occupied his chair from 1893-1919 and also practised as a public analyst, enjoyed unusual fame in having his signature printed with the certificate of analysis on every bottle of H.P. Sauce—a Birmingham product. Much earlier, the horse trams in Birmingham had carried an advertisement for "Horsfall's Invalid Port—specially recommended by Dr Bostock Hill."

Edward Malins was the grandfather of the present J M Malins, Honorary Professor of Medicine.

RIGHT: Section K (Botany) of the 1913 British Association Meeting, held in Birmingham. It includes three successive Mason Professors of Botany: G S West (1909-19) R H Yapp (1919-29) W Stiles (1929-51). Also included is Dr Marie Stopes, who by her advocacy of birth control achieved a notoriety which would be surprising today. Her son, Dr H V Stopes-Roe, is a senior lecturer in the Department of Extra-mural Studies.

Prof. BULLER. Dr. GORDON. M. J. LEGOE. T. WHITEHEAD. Miss JEPPS. Dr. DARBISHIRE. Dr. FARROW.
Dr. M. C. STOPES. Prof. M. J. BENSON. F. T. BROOKS. Miss L. J. CLARKE. Miss BAINSOF. C. G. P. LAIDLAW. H. H. THOMAS.
Miss MITCHELL. Mr. CROMPTON. R. Miss ADAMSON. Miss F. N. CHEESMAN.
Miss SAMUEL. Miss HUME. Miss WIGGLESWORTH. R. C. DAVIE. Mr. N. CHEESMAN.
Dr. BAYLISS-ELLIOTT. Miss WORTHAM. W. N. JONES. Miss BURCH. P. H. ALLEN.
Miss HALKET. Miss M. C. RAYNER. Mrs. MOSS. Col. RAWSON. Miss BAKER.
Mrs. THODAY. Dr. ELLIS. Dr. R. GATES. Mrs. HORNE. Dr. HORNE. Miss E. M. POULTON. Dr. WOODHEAD.
D. THODAY (Sec) Miss PERTZ. Miss SAUNDERS. W. WEST. W. B. BRIERLEY. Dr. H. C. J. GWYNNE-VAUGHAN. Dr. T. G. HILL. Dr. DE FRAINE. Dr. DELF.
Prof. GWYNNE-VAUGHAN (Rec) Dr. C. E. MOSS (Sec) W. STILES. G. C. DRUCE. Mrs. SCOTT. W. B. GROVE (Loc. Sec) Miss WELSFORD. Prof. WEISS.
Prof. WEST. Prof. YAPP. Dr. O. STAPF. Prof. J. REINKE. Miss E. SARGANT (Pres) Dr. SCOTT. Prof. OLIVER.

A special congregation was held on Thursday 12 September 1913 to confer honorary degrees on five distinguished foreign visitors to the British Association Meeting, which took place that year in Birmingham under the presidency of Sir Oliver Lodge. Four of them are shown in this photograph taken outside the Great Hall. STANDING, L TO R: R W Wood, Professor of Experimental Physics in the Johns Hopkins University, Baltimore; Professor H A Lorentz of Leyden; Dr Svante Arrhenius, Director of the Nobel Institute of Physics, Stockholm. SEATED: Sir Oliver Lodge, Principal of the University; Mme Sklodowska Curie; Sir Gilbert Barling, Vice-Chancellor.

In presenting them for their degrees Sir Oliver described Mme Curie as the discoverer of radium and the greatest woman of science of all time; Arrhenius as "one of the most prominent founders of physical chemistry, the principles of which he has even applied with singular success to some of the most subtle phenomena of organic life"; Lorentz as "one whose name will forever be associated with the nascent electrical theory of matter"; Wood as a prolific experimentalist, notably in his work on the structure of molecules and his application of photography to the geology of the moon.

The fifth graduate, Dr Franz Keibel, Professor of Anatomy in the University of Freiburg, was honoured as the leading authority on the development of man and the embryology of vertebrates.

After twenty years as Professor of Surgery and seven as Dean of Medicine, Gilbert Barling had recently resigned his academic posts, following the death of C G Beale, to take on the unpaid job of Vice-Chancellor—then still a lay office, equivalent to the present one of Pro-Chancellor. For the next twenty years he was to render services which were outstanding even by the high standards to which the University had grown accustomed, and like so many successful consultants—now as then—he returned a generous measure of his private earnings to the University.

In the two years before the first World War the University lost four of its founding fathers by death or retirement: C G Beale, Lapworth, Poynting and Joseph Chamberlain. Those who remained saw the war through, but by the end of 1919 Lodge himself, Sonnenschein, Heath, Frankland, Adrian Brown, Leith (Pathology), Saundby and Carter (Medicine) and Bostock Hill had all gone. It was the end of an era—of that unique half-century during which men of wisdom, not least the Birmingham professoriate, held that ignorance was the sole impediment to unlimited improvement of the human condition. (It was also the beginning of a half-century at the end of which man's highest hope is not paradise, but survival.)

August 1914 opened with the occupation of the buildings at Edgbaston by the 1st Southern General Hospital, which in the course of the war treated 125,000 cases. University House became a nurses' home. The Army claimed two former adjutants of the OTC, Colonel Loring and Major Christie—both dead by the following February—and Sgt-Major Moran, of whom General Sir William Slim, receiving an honorary degree thirty-four years later, was to say: "He taught me the whole art of war". Barling was gazetted Lieut-Colonel and went to France as consultant surgeon to the British Expeditionary Force.

The applied science departments squeezed into the Municipal Technical School in Suffolk Street, leaving behind their modern machine tools—to be sold off by the Government in 1916 to firms engaged in war production. For public consumption Sir Oliver Lodge spoke of such seeming irrelevancies as the need of a women's refectory and an additional lectureship in ancient history, while privately occupying himself and his science professors with more pressing problems of wireless telegraphy, tank design, light alloys for aircraft, poison gas and explosives. The arts and commerce professors manned committees and tribunals helping to direct the civilian war effort, or engaged in propaganda and counter-espionage.

Academic development did not cease. The Arts Faculty, which had become the largest in student numbers by 1913 and was to remain so until well after the war, introduced honours degrees. Latin ceased to be compulsory for medical students. Birmingham Chamber of Commerce raised £10,000 for a Chair of Russian. The first steps were taken towards establishing a Joint Matriculation Board with Manchester, Liverpool, Leeds and Sheffield.

In all 200 students and 54 staff had joined up by the end of 1914, half of them as officers. Professor Chatelain, who had succeeded Bèvenot, died for La Patrie; his lecturer M. Demey survived and rejoined the staff after the War. Dr Intze, assistant lecturer in German, had gone home to Heidelberg for the long vacation taking with him two students, Alexander McGeoch and Professor Turner's son Thomas Henry, to improve their German. Intze ended up as a captain on the Russian front and the two students spent the war in Ruhleben internment camp.

By the death of Sir Charles Holcroft—who was still its principal benefactor—the University came into possession of his considerable collection of Silurian fossils, garnered over many years from Dudley Castle Hill, Wren's Nest, Sedgley and Walsall, where his employees worked the limestone for use as a flux in Black Country blast furnaces. It is still a valued possession of the Geology Department.

Almost as notable, in a rather different way, was the Anatomy Department's first acquisition by bequest of a cadaver—that of Archdeacon Colley, Rector of Stockton, Warwickshire. This eccentric cleric (Rugby and Oxford) had once rounded off even-song by lying in a glass-topped coffin, the effect of which on the night's takings is not recorded. In anticipation of his demise he had written to Dr William Wright—the same who had carried the borrowed mace in the 1901 degree congregation—thus:

Please again tell me what I should do about giving in a letter or other formal disposal of my mortal remains, to be brought under my hand with my coffined corpse, particulars of what I should write as to mental idiosyncrasies, line of thought, bend of disposition, likes and dislikes, whatever else may be useful when the top of my skull, as we arranged, shall be sawn off to enable exploration to be made, that it may be known if I am, or have been, any more mad than other people.

I should further like you to tell me if, at the cost of my estate, the arrangements mentioned can be undertaken by the University, and if my bones, strongly wired together as a skeleton, labelled as I have directed, placed in my hall parlour or the Psychic Museum at Leamington, or kept for my son until his return to England from India.

In his reply Dr Wright said:

We will be quite sure that you are dead. Letter re your temperament etc. may be forwarded direct to me. Please let me know if there is anything further you do not understand. Trusting you are quite well (that's funny, isn't it?)

The Rector died of heart failure during a Church Congress at North Ormesby, Yorkshire, and was despatched by rail next day to the Anatomy Department—whose rule of strict confidentiality precludes completion of the story.

The City Council reduced its grant to £13,000 for the duration, and in 1917, soon after Neville Chamberlain had relinquished the Lord Mayoralty to enter Parliament, a Councillor Hallas successfully moved that payment be suspended "until the University agrees to discharge any pre-war unnaturalised German professor on its salaried staff". This distasteful motion was aimed at Karl Wichmann, who became a British subject after war broke out; he gallantly solved the University's dilemma by resigning his chair of German and settling in Oxford.

On 11 November 1918 Professor Wace Carlier was lecturing to an inattentive audience in the Physiology Theatre at Edmund Street. The penknife that speared his notes to the desk lacked its usual hypnotic effect, for all over the City bells were ringing. At last he accepted defeat with the memorable words "You had better go out" and the physiology class joined the great crowd in Victoria Square celebrating the signing of the Armistice.

On another floor 18-year-old Jessie Pullen★ was still working at 8 pm, and when a fellow clerk looked out of the window Sir Gilbert Barling said sharply: "Your attention should be this way, not that". The secretarial staff were preparing for the installation next day of Lord Robert Cecil as Chancellor.

Thus ended the first Great War for Birmingham University.

★Subsequently Mrs Jessie Brake, Deputy Registrar, who served under six Registrars and five Principals before her retirement in 1960.

The Great Hall as a hospital ward, its ornate electric light globes replaced by clusters of cheap conical shades. In the Hospital magazine *Southern Cross* a wag captioned it "The palace at Sinaia, the King of Roumania's summer residence in the Carpathian Mountains".

Every part of the University was utilised, mainly as wards. Marquees were erected in front of the Great Hall, and the Harding Library became a chapel. Patients who had earned decorations for bravery were wheeled outside for an open-air ceremony.

ABOVE: Nurses walking along University Road under the matron's sharp eye. The cast iron posts and chains can still be seen outside the Postgraduate Centre and on the south side of University Square.

OPPOSITE: Nurses in occupation of University House.

These and the photographs on the following pages were taken by the Birmingham photographer, Sir Benjamin Stone, MP for Birmingham East.

74

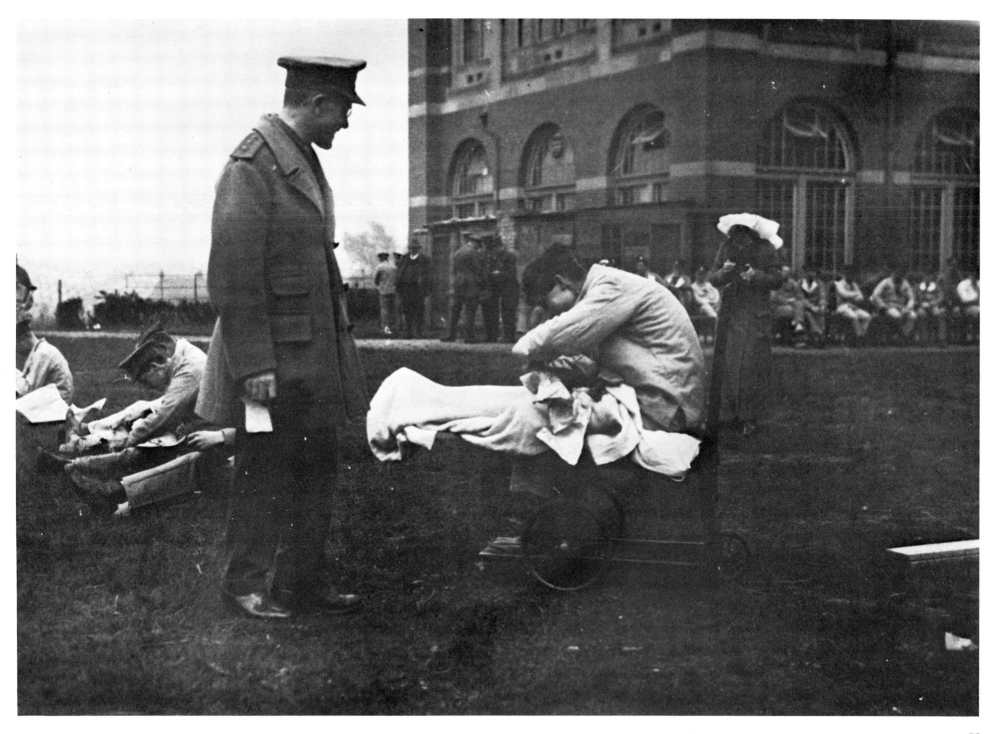

LEFT: The predominantly female Guild of Undergraduates Council 1915-16. Gladys Boone the President (BA 1916, MA 1917) went to Columbia University as first holder of the scholarship founded to commemorate Rose Sidgwick, Margery Fry's friend. She stayed in America, wrote *The Trade Union History of the Women's Clothing Industry in America*, taught industrial relations at Bryn Mawr College and the Carnegie Institute of Technology, finally became Professor of Economic History at Sweet Briar College, Virginia.

The Rose Sidgwick Scholarship is still awarded annually, alternating between a British and an American graduate.

RIGHT: The 1918-19 Faculty of Commerce. A contemporary caption names them as follows. FRONT, L TO R: Bladwell, Raby, Popovitch, Tate, Falconer, Bradbury, Cotton. SEATED: Willmore, Mendoza, Professor Martineau, The Dean (Professor Sir William Ashley), Professor Kirkaldy, Docker, Toon. BEHIND THEM: Newey, Davis, Millner, Lim, Clegg, Clarke, Harman, Winnall. REAR: White, Cousins, Cryer, Allen, Willard, Ensor, Atkins, de Geus, Margrett, Ottewell, Wilton, Milligan, Dane.

Many were British and Allied ex-servicemen studying on Government grants. E A WHITE became London manager of Archibald Kenrick and Sons. D COUSINS went into merchant banking and published several textbooks before succeeding Martineau as Professor of Accounting. H F ATKINS became Rector of Church Lench; A J FALCONER a director of Broadcast Relay Services; L J CLARKE a silk manufacturer and President of Coventry Chamber of Trade; F S MILLIGAN warden of a docks hostel at Liverpool.

W N CRYER received the OBE as Chief Commissioner of the National Savings Committee; G C ALLEN became a Professor of Economics in London University and adviser to the Government on the Japanese economy 1939-45. E R WINNALL, director of a hardware firm, commanded an anti-aircraft regiment in the last war and became principal lecturer in commerce and economics to the College of the Rhine Army.

On the same course was E C TURNER, the Birmingham accountant, who became Honorary Colonel of the University OTC.

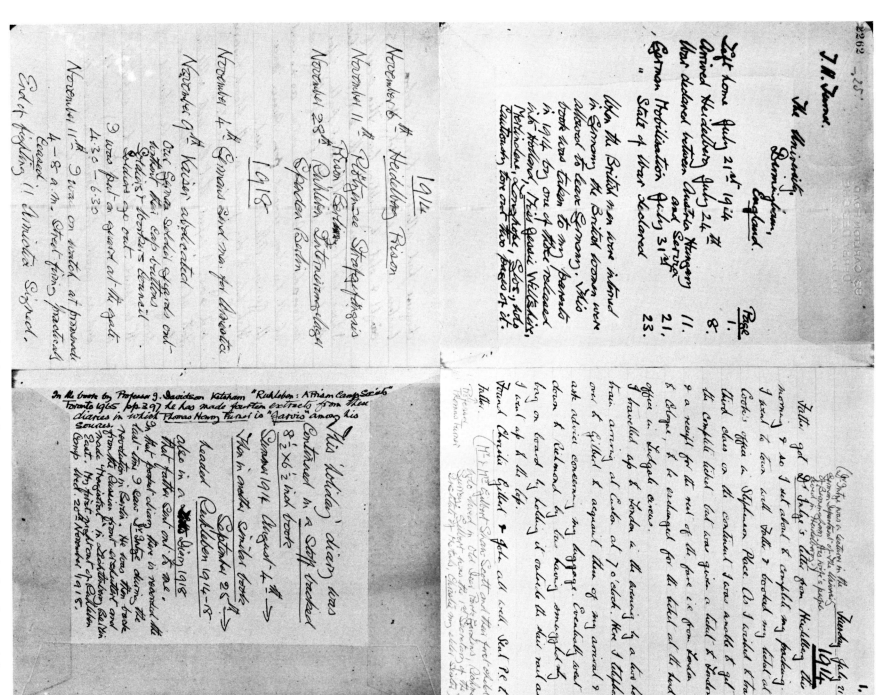

Opening and closing pages of the first of Thomas Henry Turner's internment diaries. When war ended he made his own way back to Edmund Street *via* Copenhagen and Leith. Finding Founder's Room empty, he organised a freshes' meeting for returning and ex-Forces students. Societies and sports clubs were formed, and he proposed C A F Hastilow (later a leading industrialist and member of Warwickshire County Cricket Club) as President. Turner wrote a note to *Mermaid* complaining that his apparatus, instruments, books and gowns left at Edgbaston in 1914 had all gone, graduated in metallurgy in 1920 and took his MSc in 1922. For eight years he remained as a lecturer (initially under his father) before joining the LNER, of which he was Chief Chemist and Metallurgist before becoming head of British Rail's Metallurgy Division. He remains active on committees for the prevention of corrosion and atmospheric pollution.

The pink cloud of peace

The University emerged from the first World War in a state of crisis, its student numbers doubled by the inrush of 800 grant-aided ex-Servicemen (including 70 Americans), its physical capacity halved by the continued occupation of the Edgbaston buildings, its accumulated debt £138,000. Holiday classes and evening lectures were but two of the devices employed to ease the situation, and although Edgbaston was back on stream by the next session it was another four years before the Government had fully discharged the £70,000 reparation bill. A minor compensation was the Admiralty's gift of a MAN 6-cylinder blast injection diesel engine from a German submarine; harnessed to a turbo-generator it gave excellent service, despite a sewn-up crack in the flywheel, until 1946 when it was sold.

Student numbers (excluding the diminishing proportion of part-timers) rose from some 1300 to a peak of 1600 in 1935 and thereafter declined to 1500 before the second World War. But mere numbers had not then attained their later significance, and in every other respect—teaching, research, finance, social standing, reputation abroad—the University leapt ahead. The proportion doing postgraduate work was rising. Arts gradually lost its lead in numbers, being overtaken first by Science and then by Medicine, but it was awarding more and more honours degrees under the influence of men like Ernest de Selincourt, Graeme Ritchie and Raymond Beazley. They were years of high hope.

On the first day of peace the future Viscount Cecil of Chelwood, Minister of Blockade and Under Secretary for Foreign Affairs, made his installation as Chancellor in Birmingham Town Hall the occasion for an historic speech advocating a League of Nations, carrying the University's name with his own all over the world.

Lodge retired in the following year, prophesying publicly (so many University lectures were then delivered in public) the future power of the atom to save or destroy. He was succeeded by Sir Charles Grant Robertson, an eminent Oxford historian and an outstanding administrator who never forgot his history; when Neville Chamberlain—that good friend of the University who collected subscriptions for University House in 1903 and was still guiding Sir Henry Barber's wealth in the right direction twenty years later—was giving credence to Hitler's good intentions, Grant Robertson wrote a brisk little pamphlet taking a quite opposite view. It was in keeping with the tradition of academic freedom exemplified by Lodge's opposition to Joseph Chamberlain over the Boer War, and the opposition of a later group of professors to their Chancellor, Anthony Eden, over the invasion of Suez.

Not only through lectures was contact with the community developed. There were free concerts and organ recitals; cultural associations met regularly in the evenings at Edmund Street; a joint University/WEA committee expanded extramural work; free lectures for trade unionists were initiated by J H Muirhead, Professor of Philosophy since 1897, whose name and works are commemorated by the tallest of the University's new buildings, the Muirhead Tower. Industrialists were encouraged to use the University's services by a series of lunches—to one of which a solitary gunmaker turned up. For the University's 21st birthday there was a conversazione in the Great Hall with an organist, a string band and searchlights playing on an artificial pink cloud. The Prince of Wales, whose tutor at Oxford had been Grant Robertson, spent an informal ninety minutes one evening with students and staff.

There was even money in the bank. A new appeal launched by Austen Chamberlain, then Chancellor of the Exchequer, at a public luncheon quickly raised £300,000, headed by £50,000 from an anonymous donor who could be neither Holcroft nor Strathcona, since both were dead. The great Birmingham family names—Beale, Kenrick, Cadbury, Chamberlain—were again prominent in the list, and some significant new ones like Charles Hyde (who passed to Barling his card with the pencilled message "Put me down for £10,000") and W. Waters Butler. Barling himself gave £1,000, Grant Robertson £250, and there were numerous contributions from staff, students and graduates, including the proceeds from student drama productions.

A wide spread of local companies contributed, but the big money came from the oil and mining interests—Anglo-Persian, Anglo-Saxon, Anglo-American, Viscount Cowdray, Sir Marcus Samuel. Much of it was earmarked for new developments in petroleum engineering and coal treatment, but there was plenty left for general purposes and by 1922 the University was solvent for the first time.

The Professor of Mechanical Engineering, F W Burstall, after delivering a public rebuke to Birmingham industry over working conditions, informed the world that petrol would always be too scarce and dear to compete with coal—a miscalculation that fortunately seems not to have held back the new developments. He did not err alone: the Principal predicted a drop in student numbers for 1955.

Photographs linking many of the new buildings with their principal donors have unfortunately disappeared—Sir William Waters Butler with the new Biology and Brewing Block (now Law), Sir Charles Hyde with the Students' Union, A E Hills (tube manufacturer, of Four Oaks) with the Hills Chemistry building of 1936, Edward Cadbury with St Francis Hall, Lord Nuffield with the new Physics laboratory of 1939.

The biggest building development was the new Medical School adjacent to the Queen Elizabeth Medical Centre. The Queen's and General teaching hospitals amalgamated as the United Birmingham Hospital and planned the biggest hospital complex in Europe, raising by public appeal £1¼m of which a sixth was earmarked for the Medical School. The University provided an additional £60,000, and the School was opened in 1938. But at one stage, according to Stanley Barnes (then Dean of Medicine) the scheme was nearly wrecked by Grant Robertson's irrepressible loquacity in committee.

Academic developments between the wars were many: the Faculty of Law, the Research Committee, the Barber Institute, and thirteen new professorships (still two short of Joseph Chamberlain's goal forty years earlier) including Russian, Italian, and Applied Mathematics, now Mathematical Physics.

To this last chair came in 1937, the year of Grant Robertson's retirement, a brilliant young mathematician from Cambridge, Rudolf Peierls; and at the same time, from Lord Rutherford's team at Cambridge, a new young Poynting Professor of Physics, Marcus Oliphant, of such importance that a £60,000 building had to be erected specially for him, to house also his even more expensive cyclotron. It was a remarkable coincidence, the simultaneous arrival of these two men who (with others) were destined eight years later to—literally—shake the world.

Lloyd George, who had led the nation to victory in war, was still Prime Minister when he came to Edgbaston on Saturday 5 February 1921 to receive an honorary LLD from the Vice-Chancellor, Sir Gilbert Barling—the Chancellor having sent an apology which did not specify the cause of his absence.

Earlier, at the Town Hall, Lloyd George delivered a powerful 'Germany must pay' speech to loud applause—in contrast with his reception there twenty years earlier when he had left by a back door wearing policeman's uniform to escape the wrath of Joseph Chamberlain's supporters.

Standing beside Lloyd George is Grant Robertson, and FAR RIGHT George H Morley, who was Secretary of Mason College and the University from 1880 to 1924. Morley's retirement dinner was a big occasion. Mrs Carnegie (formerly Mrs Joseph Chamberlain) and Sir Oliver Lodge sent messages, Sir Henry Fowler was present as a former Mason College student, and a cheque for £1,250 raised by subscription was handed over.

At the extreme left of the picture is the Vice-President of the Guild of Undergraduates, Dorothy K Jeyes (BSc 1914, MB ChB 1922, MD 1926) who subsequently became Mrs Flint and was in practice at Abingdon.

The next eight photographs belong to a series taken during 1923/24. LEFT: Edmond William Wace Carlier, Professor of Physiology 1900-27, lecturing at Edmund Street. Carlier had a French father and an Anglo-French education. A series of accidents, including skull and leg fractures, kept him from school games, but in manhood he became a master of fencing, riding and gymnastics. A lifelong naturalist, president several times of the Birmingham Natural History Society, he devoted much of his writing to the histology of British animals and birds—especially the hedgehog. His main contribution to science was to discover the function of the nucleolus in fatigue. His daughter Gwendoline (MSc Chemistry 1922) became biochemist to the Birmingham Skin Hospital and wrote the *Diamond Jubilee of the Guild of Graduates*.

Arthur R. Ling, Professor of Brewing 1920-31, taking a degree class in Biochemistry of Fermentation. Under his influence the Brewing School joined with Botany and Zoology under a Board of Biological Studies.

Of the students shown here, R G L Beazley (SECOND FROM LEFT, FRONT ROW, PARTLY HIDDEN) got a First and a PhD, but left biochemistry for the Church and became Vicar of Boscastle, Cornwall; A G Norman (SECOND FROM LEFT, SECOND ROW) became Professor of Botany and Vice-President of the University of Michigan. Other students of the period included R Churchman and J H Bushill, who became directors of Cadbury's and J Lyons respectively.

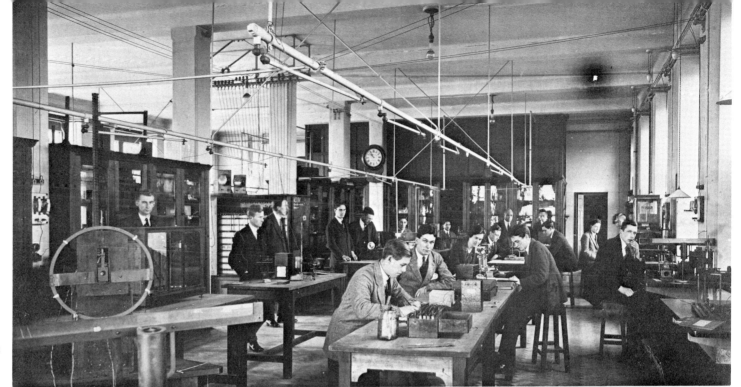

Electrical laboratory at Edgbaston

Mechanical Engineering workshop at Edgbaston

James Couper Brash, Professor of Anatomy 1922-31, in his room at Edmund Street. His many publications included anthropological studies of Anglo-Saxon burial remains, and he acquired such a reputation for his work on jaw and teeth development that the British Dental Association and other dental organisations elected him to honorary membership, while children with orthodontic problems were brought from America to see him. In the 1937 Ruxton murder case he was called to identify a skull from a photograph taken in life, and at the time of his death he had been engaged to establish a true likeness of Robert the Bruce from similar evidence for a statue to be erected on the field of Bannockburn.

A gymnastics session for teachers in training in the Department of Education. Until World War II the Department (now School, soon Faculty) was in separate divisions for men and women, each with its own head responsible to the Professor of Education.

Founder's Room at Edmund Street was for both staff and students, but only (until the last war when it became part of the University Guild Club) those of the male sex. Women had their own common room. The fact that there was also, from the early 1920s, a Mixed Common Room merely emphasised the situation.

A photograph taken 13 years later revealed the same carpet, the same furniture and the same pictures on the wall.

The Mixed Students' Common Room. Apparently it offered no alternative position to that of sitting at table—without food.

ABOVE: Professor F W Burstall and the non-academic staff of Mechanical Engineering, early 1920s.

RIGHT: Margery Fry, looking more Quakerish than in her previous photograph, came to the 1922 University House reunion to 'open' a new fountain.

Sir Charles Hyde (LEFT) inherited from his uncle John Feeney an option to buy *The Birmingham Post* and *Mail*, where he had started work as a clerk of poor means. He prospered, and being a bachelor he found outlets for his wealth in racehorses, archaeology and the University. His first gift was a lecture-ship in psychotherapy to help shell-shocked soldiers; later he helped to finance Chancellor's Hall, the former men's hostel. Of his many other benefactions the biggest was £100,000 for the present Student's Union.

The complimentary dinner to Sir William Ashley, who retired in 1925 after 24 years as Professor of Commerce and seven as Vice-Principal. Most members of Senate and Council were present. The tall figure at the top is Grant Robertson, and on his left (in order) are Alice Ashley, Barling, Ashley, Hugh Morton (University Treasurer) and Sir Frank Tillyard, Professor of Commercial Law who had succeeded Ashley as Dean two years earlier.

The dark haired lady with her back to the camera is Countess Linetta Palamidessi de Castelvecchio, first Professor of Italian, who later married the Vicar of Four Oaks, Canon R D Richardson.

"The function of the Faculty of Commerce" Ashley said "is to make business intellectually more interesting and by so doing help the young man to carry an alert mind through the dull years of necessary subordination to detail". He expressed a hope that the 'great applied science departments' would provide Commerce students with some instruction in technology, and some years later mechanical engineering was included as an option in the BCom course; but few students enrolled, and it was dropped. Since then however there have been introduced 4-year double honours courses (BSc & BCom).

The Medical School celebrated its Centenary in December 1925, taking the date from the first lessons in anatomy given by William Sands Cox at his father's Birmingham house. Honorary degrees were conferred on (L TO R ABOVE) Emeritus Professor Priestley Smith, Sir Humphry Rolleston (President of the Royal College of Physicians), Sir Donald MacAlister (Vice-Chancellor of Glasgow University) and Neville Chamberlain (then Minister of Health) who spoke at length on the need for more research into cancer, dental caries and mental health. The others in the foreground are the Lord Mayor, the Principal (Grant Robertson) and the Vice-Chancellor (Sir Gilbert Barling).

Priestley Smith had been retired nine years, but he was still doing experimental and research work. He had been Professor of Ophthalmology from 1897 to 1913, but back in 1879 he had won the Jacksonian Prize for his essay on *Glaucoma* since when honours had showered upon him.

That evening there was a reception for 2000 in the Great Hall and an exhibition which included the submarine engine and the Holcroft fossils. This was followed by dancing, and for non-dancers a music recital by the Muriel Tookey Trio.

Viscount Chelmsford, ex-Viceroy of India and future Warden of All Souls, came in November 1926 to open a new Coal Treatment Laboratory and was greeted with the usual sartorial flippancies (often half-hearted) which students in those days of the flapper and the Charleston felt it their duty to provide.

Immediately behind him is K Neville Moss, who came as a mining student from Queen Mary's Grammar School, Walsall, in 1911 and was Professor of Mining 1922-42. He had acquired a knowledge of mining in many countries and played a leading part in the re-organisation of the British industry. The

industry's Doncaster Laboratory, under Dr J S Haldane, had been transferred (through the influence of Cadman) to Birmingham, which became a leading centre of research into coal utilisation and the conversion of coal into oil. This latter work was nullified by the rapidly increasing supply and falling price of

crude oil from the Middle East (contrary to Burstall's prediction) but the staff put their knowledge to good use in the 'gas producers' that kept public transport moving in World War II.

Sir John Cadman returned in 1926 to the University he had only recently left to open the new building of the Department of Oil Engineering, his own idea. He is seen on the right of the picture FAR LEFT with (CENTRE) Professor A W Nash, head of the department 1924–42, and the Principal, Grant Robertson. Also shown are the oil derricks, the site of which

is now West Car Park, and the building itself, now an annexe of the main Chemical Engineering Building.

ABOVE: guests at the opening, walking past the old power station (since replaced by the present Mechanical Engineering building) led by Grant Robertson and Cadman.

Cadman had suggested detaching

petroleum engineering from mining and forming a separate department, foreseeing the conflict of interest that would otherwise ensue. Under this arrangement the Department of Oil Engineering (now Chemical Engineering) grew to be the biggest of the engineering departments—notably under Professor 'Fred' Garner (1942–60) who had spent twenty years

working for the leading oil companies in Britain and America before returning to the University where he took his first degree. He had been chief chemist at Fawley as early as 1921, and later in the course of introducing quality control for Esso he pioneered the use of knock-rating which led to the statutory 'star' classification of petrol today.

The History Students' Fellowship in 1927 with (CENTRE) Sir Raymond Beazley, Professor of History 1909-33, and Lady Beazley. Next to her is Dorothy Sutcliffe, who was on the staff 1919-49 and married Philip Styles, Reader in English history, who retired in 1970 after forty years' service.

Beazley's *Henry the Navigator* (1895) was the prelude to many major works including *Dawn of Modern Geography* and *History of Russia*. A close friend of the Labour statesmen Philip Snowden and Lord Jowett, he was an impressive figure in his hard-brimmed hat and yellow waistcoat, swinging a silver-knobbed cane. But he failed in his ambition of becoming an ambassador, and after retirement formed an active admiration for the Nazis which resulted in ostracism by his fellow Birmingham magistrates.

The elderly lady is Miss Dormer Harris, part-time lecturer and authority on the history of Coventry. Seated on the pillar (LEFT) is Lilian Seckler, who took first class honours in 1928 and became the wife of H A Cronne, now Emeritus Professor of Medieval History.

The absentees (it was in the middle of finals) included G E Taylor, who became Head of the Institute of Pacific Affairs in the University of Washington and a close friend of Senator Hubert Humphrey.

Stanley Baldwin, then Prime Minister, came in 1927 to open the new building for Zoology, Botany and Brewing & Biochemistry which linked the Harding Library with the Frankland Chemistry building, completing that part of the Aston Webb design, and also the extensions to Chancellor's Hall, the residence for men students in Augustus Road.

After being welcomed by the Chancellor, Viscount Cecil (RIGHT) he received an honorary degree and submitted to the customary student frolic, riding in a chariot that echoed the current film spectacular *Ben Hur* and being presented with a giant cherrywood pipe—his affection for the weed being well known.

Baldwin recalled his days as a metallurgy student at Mason College under Thomas Turner and after tributes to the University's benefactors, in particular Sir William Waters Butler and Sir Charles Hyde, he introduced a sly reference to the City's contribution. The Government, he said, was now providing £60-70,000 a year, the City £15,000 and other local authorities £4,000. "I am not competent to judge whether these subscriptions are adequate from every point of view—I offer no opinion—but I cannot help being enormously impressed by the way Leeds and Yorkshire have helped their great local university." Three years later the City raised its contribution to £26,000, and the other authorities theirs to £7,000.

Leaders of the law received honorary degrees at a special congregation on 30 June 1928 marking the foundation of the Law Faculty. This picture on the steps of the Great Hall shows (L TO R, non-honorary graduates in italics)—
FRONT: Lord Hewart (Lord Chief Justice), Lord Hailsham (Lord Chancellor), *Viscount Cecil (Chancellor of the University), the Lord Mayor (Alderman A H James)*, Lord Atkin of Aberdovey,

Mr Justice McCardie (a Birmingham man). REAR: Sir William Holdsworth (Vinerian Professor of English Law, Oxford), *Sir Charles Grant Robertson (Principal)*, Sir Richard Pinsent (Birmingham Solicitor and ex-President of the Law Society), *Professor C E Smalley-Baker (first Professor of Law), Sir Gilbert Barling* and *Hugh Morton (Treasurer)*.

A Department of Legal Studies headed by

Professor (later Sir) Frank Tillyard had been set up in 1923 to meet the requirements of the Solicitors Act 1922. Subsequently Sir Henry Barber, a Birmingham solicitor who had retired many years earlier and become Master of the South Oxfordshire Hunt, wrote to Neville Chamberlain offering £20,000 to found the Barber Chair of Law, and Smalley-Baker was appointed. Tillyard continued to teach

commercial law as he had done (in the Faculty of Commerce) since 1904.

The revision of the Charter to include the new faculty "took nearly as long to revise as the Book of Common Prayer" observed Grant Robertson.

Sir Henry Barber died in 1927, but his generosity continued through his widow, Dame Hattie Barber, who sought advice from her trusted friends Sir Charles Grant Robertson and Sir Gilbert Barling on the disposal of her wealth. The result was the Barber Trust,which provided us with the Barber Institute of Fine Arts.

Each year until her death in 1932 Lady Barber invited staff and students of the Law Faculty to spend a day in June at her home, Culham Court, Henley-on-Thames. She provided lunch and boats, and it was generally regarded as a good outing.

The above photograph records the event of 17 June 1929. On Lady Barber's left is Smalley-Baker, and behind them stands George Grove, who later became a successful Queen's Counsel, at the same time serving the University as part-time Professor of Conveyancing and Equity and, for two years, Dean of the Faculty.

On the extreme left, front row, is T H Parkinson who became Town Clerk of Birmingham; sixth from the left is G G Burkitt, later Clerk of Oxfordshire County Council. At the far rear (LEFT) is W H Tilley QC, a leading counsel in property law.

Among those present at the Baldwin degree congregation had been Sir Fitzroy and Lady Anstruther-Gough-Calthorpe, and the occasion inspired them to make the third and largest (41 acres) gift of Calthorpe land to the University. It extended the northern boundary from University Road to Pritchatts Road and the canal, providing sites for most of the subsequent buildings.

It also presented the opportunity for an impressive Central Avenue 330 yards long by 15 yards wide leading in a straight line from Pritchatts Road to the Great Hall, via the existing Harding Library gates and the arch of the Chamberlain Tower. This irresistible touch of grandeur was initiated with a massive set of elegant wrought-iron entrance gates, the work of the Birmingham Guild of Handicraft, hung on neo-Egyptian pillars with twin gatehouses to match.

The gates were formally opened in May 1930 by Lady Calthorpe, on which occasion the above photograph was taken. Twin gatehouses and a fine avenue of Lombardy poplars flanked by Wheatley elms followed. But after the war less grandiose concepts intervened; the fate of the Central Avenue may be seen in later pages.

The Jubilee of the opening of Mason College
was celebrated in October 1930 with a special
honorary degrees congregation. Lady Astor,
first woman MP, feminist and teetotaller, was
the star turn. She is seen here after the ceremony
laughing with Sir Oliver Lodge, who had been
retired eleven years. On the right are Lord Cecil
and Sir Austen Chamberlain. The wing-collar,
orchid and *pince-nez* belong to Sir William
Waters Butler; behind him are C T Onions,
who had now become chief editor of the
Oxford Dictionary, and Canon J E H Blake,
Librarian of Worcester Cathedral and the first
enrolled student of Mason College, whose
father was Mason's friend Dr J Gibbs Blake.

Lady Astor and Onions both received
honorary degrees; Chamberlain had been
honoured earlier. Among the many other
graduands were Adrian Boult, who had just
been lured away from the City of Birmingham
Symphony Orchestra by the BBC, and Alderman W A Cadbury whose family had just
given 150 acres on the other side of the canal
for the newly projected Queen Elizabeth
Medical Centre and the University's new
Medical School.

There was a reception in the evening with
dancing—there always seemed to be dancing—
in the Great Hall. And again the non-dancers
(or the wall-flowers?) were catered for with a
musical recital by Miss Dorothy Silk and
Mr Michael Mullinar.

On the steps of the new Medical School, 14 July 1938. The blessing is being pronounced by Dr E W Barnes, Bishop of Birmingham and eldest brother of Dr Stanley Barnes, who was Dean of the Faculty of Medicine 1931–41 and had been mainly responsible for the new Medical School.

On either side of the Bishop are the Duke and Duchess of Gloucester. The Duke performed the formal opening on behalf of King George VI, who was prevented by illness from attending but paid a visit to the School in the following March.

Neville Chamberlain, then Prime Minister,

and Mrs Chamberlain are on the right of the picture. At the extreme left is Sir Charles Grant Robertson, the Vice-Chancellor.

Bishop Barnes was the eldest of four distinguished sons of a Birmingham chief inspector of schools. He was a radical in religion as well as in politics, and attacked

Sacramentalism as vigorously as he advocated pacifism, socialism, and birth control.

The University conferred honorary degrees on Stanley Barnes in 1942 and on the Bishop in 1953, the year of his retirement.

The coming of World War II was marked by the building of a 14in blast wall round the equestrian statue of George I. Mere mortals sought shelter in the model coal mine if they were near enough. For those at Edmund Street there were sandbags.

Entry to arts and commerce was mainly for the unfit; science and engineering students faced a four-term year with 257 hours' military training. Patriot though he was, the Vice-Chancellor (Sir Raymond Priestley) would have reserved outstanding arts students as postwar seedcorn, but Whitehall said no.

In December 1940 three high explosive bombs and a fire gutted the former Medical School area at Edmund Street, during the Vice-Chancellor's turn on firewatch. The following Easter fourteen HEs bounced across the Edgbaston campus and incendiaries showered the Medical School, but did little damage. Priestley reported, with perhaps a touch of pride, that the University had become a legitimate military target—not referring specifically to the radar that defeated the German submarines, or the atom bomb team code-named "Tube Alloys", or the particularly nasty flamethrower devised in Oil Engineering.

A native of Tewkesbury, he had come from Melbourne in 1938 with a firm commitment to *mens sana in corpore sano*, a belief that 'no university can be healthy without a strong left wing,' and the authority of having been with both Shackleton and Scott to the Antarctic. Despite opposition he introduced compulsory physical training (it included four varieties of dancing) and built a gymnasium and squash court. The flagging OTC (then STC) was revivified. There followed the Department of Physical Education, first in Britain to offer a degree course.

Lord Nuffield had been gravely offended by the clangour of handbells and the sputter of a motor-bike while receiving his honorary degree, and Priestley succeeded in abolishing these time-honoured capers. But he failed, like his predecessors, to see the University united on the Edgbaston campus. That came in 1960.

There was a rare but sharp tiff with the Guild of Graduates over the decision to drop workshop courses from the Engineering curricula. Priestley supported his professors, but the heart-searching over the content of courses has continued ever since.

Josiah Mason had a simple faith that it was only necessary to open the doors of science to transform the world. T H Huxley, wiser, cautioned him that science must go hand in hand with the humanities—a principle accepted by Joseph Chamberlain and Sonnenschein, and by Priestley in his philosophising over The Bomb. Both Chamberlain and Barling had dissociated the University from 'mere technical instruction'.

It was the explosion of knowledge, its cell-like multiplication, that now thrust these issues to the fore. What proportion of a three-year course could be spared for new specialisms? What proportion for broadening the mind—Shakespeare for the engineer, amino-acids for the linguist? Most departments answered the first question with a basic course and a choice of specialisms. The second, under the label of 'Broader' (originally 'Liberal') Education, is still in dispute.

When GCE replaced the pre-war School Certificate, Senate opposed too much specialisation in the sixth form but was out-voted by other universities. In Electrical Engineering a brave experiment was tried in 1948 by Professor A Tustin, who introduced philosophy, literature and economics into his syllabus. The idea failed to germinate, but there is now an extensive programme of Inter-Faculty Studies; broader education enthusiasts think it is not enough.

New centres and departments began offering teaching and research in inter-disciplinary, user-orientated packages. The Department of Engineering Production was launched—despite opposition from academic purists—with £112,000 from the Joseph Lucas company, and soon its offshoot, the Lucas Institute, was founded to provide residential courses for businessmen. The principle has since been extended to Materials Science, Urban and Regional Studies, Local Government, Transportation and Environmental Planning, administration in the Health Service and Social Services, Ergonomics and Low Cost Automation, and there is now a Director of Post-Experience Training. Other developments have been the Centre of West African Studies and the Centre for Russian and East European Studies (involving scientific as well as arts subjects), the Shakespeare Institute, the pioneering Institute for Judicial Administration, the Centre for Child Study, the Institute of Child Health and the Wolfson Research Centre, which concentrates on techniques of medical diagnosis.

The postwar Calendars contain many names that have become widely known. They include two Chief Scientific Advisers to the Government, Lord Zuckerman (who journeyed regularly from Whitehall to Birmingham to direct the Department of Anatomy) and his successor Sir Alan Cottrell, Birmingham graduate and former Professor of Metallurgy, besides Sir Norman Haworth, Sir Mark Oliphant and Sir Rudolf Peierls. The versatile Lancelot Hogben, whose *Mathematics for the Million* and *Science for the Citizen* were world best-sellers, switched from the chair of Zoology to that of Medical Statistics, and on reaching retirement became an honorary fellow in Linguistics. The Professor of Linguistics himself, A S C Ross found fame through the writings of Nancy Mitford with his concept of U and non-U language. This random list could be greatly extended.

Of all the students who have passed through Mason College and the University, two-thirds belong to the post-1939 era. In the last thirty years University income has risen from £277,000 to £16m, which even allowing for inflation represents a growth factor of 13. Student numbers have risen from 1700 to nearly 8000, staff from 158 to around 1100, professors from 45 to 162.

But successive vice-chancellors have felt uneasy about the growth in mere numbers. Humphrey Humphreys (1952-53) warned that the UGC grant was so geared to student numbers as to endanger our research—"a magnet to the world". Sir Robert Aitken (1953-68) foresaw that the Robbins Report might lead to "increased output of first degrees at the expense of research". His successor, Dr Robert Hunter, has repeated the warning.

So far a balance between teaching and research has been maintained by our success in attracting research grants and contracts, which have risen to £3½m in a single year. Midland people and industry have responded magnificently to three post-war appeals, one specifically for research. The medical professors—notably Stanley Barnes and Sir Arthur Thomson—have continued a tradition of remarkable generosity. So the University remains relatively fortunate in that up to a quarter of its income is from sources other than the University Grants Committee. But the contribution from local authorities, which once represented 50%, is now little more than 0.1%.

Growth meant many more buildings—an increase in floor area from 674,000 to 4m sq. ft. Under the leadership of Sir Stephen Burman (Pro-Chancellor 1955-66) and Sir Robert Aitken a simple but far reaching decision was taken to retain Sir Hugh Casson and his partner Neville Conder as site architects; this has transformed the campus into one of the finest in the country. It has a happy blend of extravagant Edwardianism (called 'Byzantine' in its day) with a whole range of brick, concrete and glass typifying successive architectural styles that flourished between 1900 and 1975; they form a harmonious whole with a real sense of place.

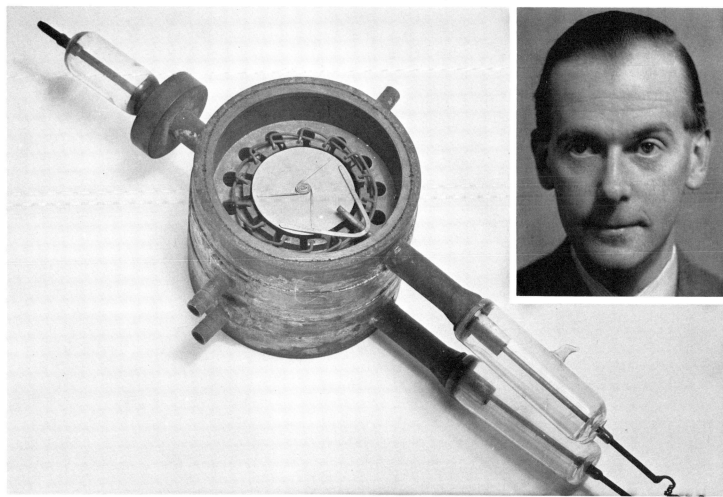

The first resonant cavity magnetron valve, which proved a decisive weapon against the submarine and the night bomber. Its inventors were a young PhD student, Henry Boot, and Dr John Randall, a member of the Physics research staff. A major improvement was subsequently made by James Sayers.

Dr Boot came from King Edward's School, Birmingham, graduating BSc 1938 and PhD 1941. He is now Senior Principal Scientific Officer, Royal Navy. Sir John Randall is an Emeritus Professor of King's College, London. Professor Sayers retired recently from the Chair of Electron Physics and Space Research.

The official American history says: "This revolutionary discovery, which we owe to a group of British physicists headed by Professor M L Oliphant of Birmingham, was the first tube capable of producing power enough to make radar feasible at wavelengths of less than 50 cm. When the Tizard mission bought one to America in 1940 they carried the most valuable cargo ever brought to our shores. It sparked the whole development of microwave radar and constituted the most important item in reverse Lease-Lend."

Boot (inset, above), Randall and Sayers received equal shares of £36,000 from the Royal Commission on Awards to Inventors in 1949.

Sir Mark Oliphant, now Governor of South Australia, is pictured (right) after receiving an honorary degree in 1950. He was Head of the Physics Department and in overall charge of radar research, but he also played an intermediary role in the early events leading to the production of the atom bomb—see next page.

RIGHT: Otto Frisch and Rudolf Peierls after receiving the American Medal of Freedom in 1946.

Frisch, with his aunt Lise Meitner, had already explained the theory of fission in the uranium nucleus. At the start of the war he came to Birmingham and lodged with Peierls (Professor of Mathematical Physics 1937-63). Together, in three typewritten pages, they calculated that a bomb could be made with uranium 235, its critical mass, how the 235 isotope could be separated, how to explode it, and the radiation dangers.

The British MAUD Committee on nuclear energy, which included three Birmingham members—Professor Oliphant, Professor Haworth and Dr P B Moon—was already aware of the explosive potential of U235. But the Frisch-Peierls paper had a profound effect upon the speed and direction of A-bomb research. None of the conclusions had been tested experimentally, but they proved remarkably accurate—and Peierls made another important contribution with an improved method of isotope separation, gaseous diffusion.

In 1943 Moon, Frisch, Peierls and others from Birmingham joined the American bomb project at Los Alamos. Another group under Oliphant worked at Berkeley, California.

Moon, who in 1935 had demonstrated the "thermalization" of neutrons which was vital for nuclear power, subsequently became Poynting Professor of Physics. Frisch became Jacksonian Professor of Natural Philosophy at Cambridge. Sir Rudolf Peierls became Wykeham Professor of Physics at Oxford.

After the War Birmingham became a Mecca for theoretical physicists. The 'shrine' was an army hut in which Professor Peierls's department was housed; it has since been replaced by the Watson Building.

RIGHT: Professor Peierls and staff about 1948.

FAR RIGHT, TOP: An international conference at Birmingham in 1948 being addressed by Professor Oliphant. The man with his hand in his pocket is J Robert Oppenheimer who had led the American atom research at Los Alamos; on his right is Professor P B Moon.

FAR RIGHT: Two Nobel Laureates, Paul Dirac and Wolfgang Pauli with Professor Peierls in 1953. The army hut is in the background.

From 1939, before the bomb was considered a serious possibility, the Department of Chemistry under Professor Sir Norman Haworth was doing pioneer work for the British Atomic Energy project. This research, in association with ICI, soon became directly relevant to the bomb project. Two years earlier Haworth had received the Nobel Prize for Chemistry; he had produced the world's first synthetic vitamin—Vitamin C.

The above photograph of the research team in 1941/42 shows Haworth in the centre and (on his left, one removed) his deputy Maurice Stacey, who later became Mason Professor of Chemistry.

One of their tasks in conjunction with ICI was to produce metallic uranium, an essential for the chemistry of Uranium 235, and this they successfully achieved. The first 30 pounds of it were produced by J Wilkinson (third from left, back row).

A later task was to synthesise an entirely new series of carbon fluorine compounds which were necessary for the handling of the extremely reactive gaseous compound, uranium hexafluoride, used in separating Uranium 235.

The photograph shows, left to right— FRONT: W J Hickenbottom; Colonel F W Pinkard; S R Carter; Haworth; L Bircumshaw; Stacey; Fred Smith. MIDDLE: A D Booth; G D Thomas; W G M Jones; Sybil James, now a Reader in Biochemistry; Ethel Teece; Ray Boyle; Leslie F Thomas, now Senior Lecturer in Chemistry. BACK: G F Claringbull; H Geoffrey Bray, now Reader in Biochemistry; L F Wiggins; J Wilkinson; K F Chackett; W K R Musgrave.

Professor Musgrave, now at Durham, is one of several members of the Department who have founded their own schools of fluorine chemistry. Sir Gordon Claringbull is Director of the British Museum (Natural History).

Anthony Eden, who had resigned as Foreign Secretary in 1938 in protest against Neville Chamberlain's appeasement policy, became the University's third Chancellor in succession to Viscount Cecil of Chelwood. They had much in common, for Eden was a great protagonist of the League of Nations and in the early thirties was a familiar and popular figure in the capitals of Europe when he was trying to make the League an effective force for peace.

He was the "one strong young figure" who, as Churchill wrote later, stood up in 1938 against "long, dismal, drawling tides of drift and surrender." During Churchill's wartime leadership he had been Foreign Secretary and Leader of the House.

At his installation in November 1945 honorary degrees were conferred on (ABOVE) the wartime leaders with whom he had worked.

LEFT TO RIGHT, FRONT: Field Marshal Lord Alexander (Supreme Allied Commander, Mediterranean), George Hall (Colonial Secretary), Eden, René Massigli (French Ambassador), Sir Ronald Campbell (British Minister in Washington).

REAR: Vincent Massey (High Commissioner for Canada), Lord Cunningham (First Sea Lord and Chief of Naval Staff), Lord Portal (Chief of Air Staff), Viscount Cranborne (resigned with Eden in 1938—became Earl of Salisbury).

At the ceremony in the Great Hall the Chancellor was invited to assume office by Edmund Phipson Beale, son of Charles Gabriel Beale and Pro-Chancellor 1939-47.

The University celebrated its jubilee in 1950 with a magnificent banquet at the Grand Hotel followed by a special congregation at which honorary degrees were conferred upon (LEFT TO RIGHT, ABOVE) E P Beale, Pro-Chancellor; Sir Peter Bennett, MP, Chairman of Joseph Lucas; Princess Alice of Athlone, grand-daughter of Queen Victoria and Chancellor of the University of the West Indies; H B Chatwin, President of the Birmingham Archaeological Society; Brigadier Anstruther-Gough-Calthorpe, life tenant of the Calthorpe Estate; Lewis Douglas, American Ambassador; Francis Brett Young, the novelist who had qualified in medicine at the University and whose collected papers are now held in the library; Sir Barry Jackson, founder of the Birmingham Repertory Theatre. Also honoured was C D Medley, chairman of the Barber Trustees.

TOP LEFT: This expedition to the Arctic Circle of Norway in 1949 was organised by seven geography students and accompanied by Dr G T Warwick, now Reader in Geomorphology.

LEFT TO RIGHT, subsequent career in brackets: James Ridsdale (Birmingham headmaster), J N Jackson (Professor in Ontario), Derek Hull (headmaster), R G Hunt (master K E S Camp Hill), J W Sweetman (Malay Civil Service), E T Stringer (Scientific Director, Edgbaston Observatory), G T Warwick, D H Renhard (mathematics lecturer, Bromsgrove).

LEFT: The University's first three public orators, left to right, were Professor Thomas Bodkin (Director, Barber Institute) 1946-50, R L Graeme Ritchie (Professor of French) 1934-46, and O Hood Phillips (Professor of Jurisprudence) 1950-62, The occasion was the conferring of an honorary degree on Professor Ritchie in 1952.

ABOVE: The 1950 annual meeting of the British Association for the Advancement of Science was held in Birmingham, and brought together these three successive occupants of the Mason Chair of Geology—LEFT TO RIGHT, L J Wills (1932-49,) W S Boulton (1913-32) and F W Shotton (1949-74).

Sir Raymond Priestley, Vice-Chancellor
1938-52, from the portrait by Middleton Todd.
He had been with Shackleton to the Antarctic
in 1907 and was a member of Scott's last
expedition, of which he wrote an account.
He encouraged outdoor pursuits and brought
physical education into degree courses. After
his retirement he was responsible for locating
the Earth Sciences section of the British
Antarctic Survey at the University. An outdoor
centre at Coniston Water is now being built
as a memorial bearing his name.

As leader of the West Midlands Group on
Postwar Reconstruction he involved the
University closely in local planning, leading to
the publication of *Conurbation* in 1948. The
Centre for Urban and Regional Studies owes
much to his influence.

The view (RIGHT) that will never be seen again.
This was the grand approach to the University
from Pritchatts Road that Lady Calthorpe had
inaugurated in 1930. It succumbed to new
planning ideas and ended up as the grand
approach to a rather minor car park, as
explained in the following pages.

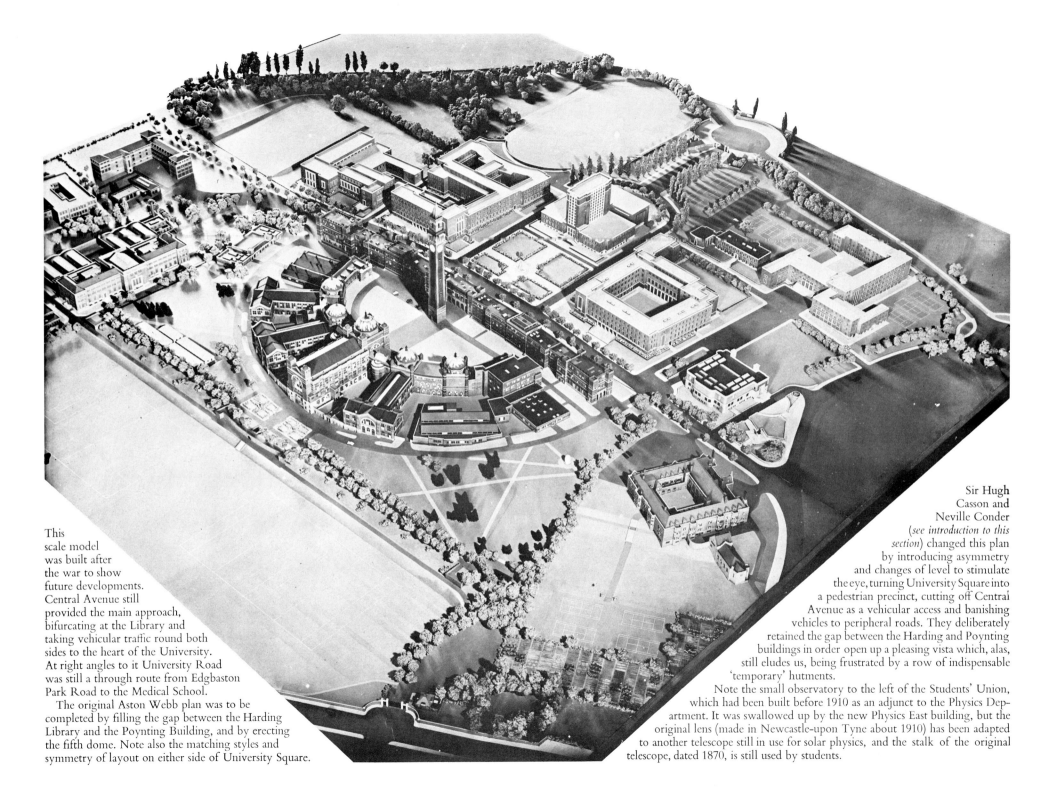

This
scale model
was built after
the war to show
future developments.
Central Avenue still
provided the main approach,
bifurcating at the Library and
taking vehicular traffic round both
sides to the heart of the University.
At right angles to it University Road
was still a through route from Edgbaston
Park Road to the Medical School.

The original Aston Webb plan was to be
completed by filling the gap between the Harding
Library and the Poynting Building, and by erecting
the fifth dome. Note also the matching styles and
symmetry of layout on either side of University Square.

Sir Hugh
Casson and
Neville Conder
(*see introduction to this
section*) changed this plan
by introducing asymmetry
and changes of level to stimulate
the eye, turning University Square into
a pedestrian precinct, cutting off Central
Avenue as a vehicular access and banishing
vehicles to peripheral roads. They deliberately
retained the gap between the Harding and Poynting
buildings in order open up a pleasing vista which, alas,
still eludes us, being frustrated by a row of indispensable
'temporary' hutments.

Note the small observatory to the left of the Students' Union,
which had been built before 1910 as an adjunct to the Physics Department. It was swallowed up by the new Physics East building, but the
original lens (made in Newcastle-upon-Tyne about 1910) has been adapted
to another telescope still in use for solar physics, and the stalk of the original
telescope, dated 1870, is still used by students.

University Square as it was earlier envisaged (ABOVE) and as it is (BELOW). The Library tower block was omitted, but a nearby off-centre site was allocated to the Muirhead Tower. Instead of the formal steps and building shown on the left of the sketch there is now the delightfully informal corner illustrated on page 111.

In their report Casson and Conder said: "We have kept in the forefront of our minds the convenience, safety and pleasures of the pedestrian. . . to stroll and converse or to walk and enjoy the pleasures of the scene have today in nearly all urban landscapes become hazardous occupations. For a University in particular this is a lamentable condition." They also remarked that they had "deliberately emasculated" University Road in order to end its popular use as a short-cut to the Queen Elizabeth Medical Centre.

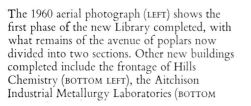

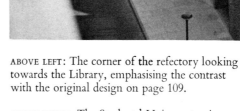

The 1960 aerial photograph (LEFT) shows the first phase of the new Library completed, with what remains of the avenue of poplars now divided into two sections. Other new buildings completed include the frontage of Hills Chemistry (BOTTOM LEFT), the Aitchison Industrial Metallurgy Laboratories (BOTTOM RIGHT) and just above these the Physics West building. Under construction are the Arts and Watson buildings, including the bridge over University Road. Staff House, the University Centre, the Muirhead Tower, the Ashley and Strathcona Buildings and the School of Education were still to come.

ABOVE LEFT: The corner of the refectory looking towards the Library, emphasising the contrast with the original design on page 109.

ABOVE RIGHT: The Students' Union extension has a broad foot-bridge linking it to the central campus. Combined with the lowered level of the road, it has the effect of subordinating motor vehicles to the pedestrian and partially concealing them. A similar arrangement exists at the rear of the Muirhead Tower and the Library.

Queen Elizabeth the Queen Mother came in May 1957 to lay the foundation stone of the new Library. She is seen above with Mr (now Sir) Stephen Burman, who was Pro-Chancellor 1955-66 during the University's crucial period of post-war expansion.

The photograph RIGHT recalls her visit nineteen years earlier to the Medical School, which George VI had been prevented by illness from opening. They are seen in the Chamberlain Museum—the King alongside Dr Stanley Barnes, Dean of Medicine, and the Queen with Dr Humphrey F Humphreys, first Professor of Dental Surgery and head of the Dental School, subsequently Vice-Chancellor 1952-53.

Queen Elizabeth II visited the University in 1963, accompanied by the Duke of Edinburgh, to view some of the new buildings. She is seen TOP LEFT with Rodney C Klevan, President of the Guild of Undergraduates, now a barrister on the Northern Circuit.

RIGHT: In the Haworth Chemistry Building, which was the first of the new buildings to depart from traditional redbrick, are (LEFT TO RIGHT) Maurice Stacey, Mason Professor of Chemistry and Head of the Department; J C Robb, Professor of Physical Chemistry; the Queen and the Duke; the Vice-Chancellor, Sir Robert Aitken.

The Royal party divided during the visit, the Duke concentrating on new engineering techniques which included explosive metal extrusion, an electronically controlled drilling machine, applications of ergonomics and the dielectric valve.

The Vale Halls of Residence. LEFT: view from the ridge looking down across the lake. RIGHT: Ridge Hall as seen from its 17-storey neighbour High Hall (not shown here).

The Vale Site had been bought on very generous terms from the Calthorpe Estate. Casson and Conder described it as "a mature, gracefully contoured and luxuriously planted piece of park land. . . the only thing missing is a sheet of water."

In 1960 Sir Bertram Waring launched our Diamond Jubilee Appeal for £1,638,250—the estimated cost of the Vale Halls scheme less £460,000 from the sale of other properties and £500,000 from the University Grants Committee—and by the end of the year it had already raised £1,400,000. The response by Midland industry was magnificent, with amounts of £150,000 each from Tube Investments and GKN and substantial sums from BMC, Cadburys, Birmingham Post and Mail and others. The Guild of Graduates raised £25,000 from members' private pockets.

The site architects got their lake, despite arguments over cost. A 3-acre area was excavated and lined with strips of plastic sheet 60-feet wide, welded together on site and anchored with a layer of gravel. A natural stream maintains the water level.

The basic arrangement of the halls is in three pairs, each containing a block for men and one for women, with common catering and social facilities. They accommodate more than 1400 students in study-bedrooms, some single and some shared.

More recently the University has used the mortgage market to build Griffin Close, a student village of 276 flats in 41 blocks off the Bristol Road; each flat houses 3-5 students. Nearby Manor House, a former Cadbury property, has been converted into a hall for 146 men students. University House, which opened under Margery Fry in 1904 as a hall for women students, is now occupied by both sexes.

Further building at The Vale will bring total University accommodation to 3,300 places.

In recent years the letting of halls during vacations has been developed as a source of income; an incidental benefit from this has been the installation of wash-hand basins in some bedrooms.

In 1966 the Senate found itself deeply divided over modifications to the Great Hall, virtually unchanged since 1909. Sir Robert Aitken reported: "The traditionalists saw the Hall as a period piece of architecture, not lacking in merit and worthy to be preserved as Aston Webb conceived it. The functionalists wanted its unfortunate acoustics improved, and by and large they won the day."

The platform was extended and tiered; Sir Aston Webb's gracious curves were partly obscured by a large overhead canopy and side panels made of aluminium with acoustic plastic infill; an amplifying system was installed. At the same time the organ was considerably improved and extended.

LEFT: The stage of the Great Hall as it was and (RIGHT) after modification—a degree ceremony being filmed by the University Television and Film Unit.

Traditionalists may find some compensation in the fact that the City of Birmingham Symphony Orchestra now uses the Great Hall for recording sessions.

The increase in number and size of degree congregations was also an argument in favour of change. Sir Raymond Priestley had referred to the heavy burden of two congregations in July; there are now six.

There was no such opposition to the sacrifice of some very fine oak woodwork during the conversion (page 118) of the Harding Library for the Faculty of Law. It was hailed in the Dean's report as "one of the most successful architectural conversions in the University." Much of the Law Faculty was then still in huts, waiting for Biology to move into the new Biology Block.

The Harding Library—before and after.

Last glimpse of Mason College, 1963. The demolition men saved the mermaid (p 143) and four armorial bearings carved in stone which have been re-erected in the covered passage between the Law Faculty and Frankland Building. A set of coins of the realm that were current in 1875 came from beneath the foundation stone and is preserved in the Library. Several desk tops from the Medical Lecture Theatre, bearing carved names that later became well known, were rescued by Dr Ben Davis of Anatomy. Of the statue of Mason seated nothing remains except a bronze casting of the head and shoulders which the City Council has erected at Erdington, near the site of his orphanage.

Sir Robert Aitken, Vice-Chancellor, with Mrs Daisy Drinkwater at the 1963 exhibition in the Library which marked the 25th anniversary of the death of her husband, John Drinkwater, the poet and dramatist. The opportunity presented by the spacious new Library for exhibitions of this kind was quickly exploited by the Librarian, Dr Kenneth Humphreys. The Library also became the home of several major collections of papers—notably of the Chamberlains (Joseph, Austen and Neville) and Lord Avon, rich in source material for future students of modern history, and of John Galsworthy, Francis Brett Young (a Birmingham medical graduate), Harriet Martineau and Sir Oliver Lodge.

LEFT: The last-ever group photograph of Guild Council, 1967-68. In the following year members decided that it was an irrelevancy.

The President is Charles Wright, and on his left is the following year's President, Ray Phillips. Seventh in the third row is Rod Playford, who became President 1970-71 and a member of the Review Body (page 123). All three were members of the "Committee of Ten" which provided the main impetus for the 1968 sit-in (see below)

Thursday 5 December 1968. This general meeting of the Guild of Undergraduates (now 'of Students') in front of the Library finally ended a one week sit-in of the Administrative Block which was unlike anything the University had ever known before. It is necessary to say 'finally' because a general meeting two days earlier had also voted to end the sit-in, but this vote was frustrated by a closely knit activist group with links in Europe and America; one leading member was a temporary assistant lecturer in Sociology.

The *causus belli* was a student proposal made early in the year for more representation in University government. Contemporary documents suggest that this had been dealt with both expeditiously and sympathetically—though it went considerably less far than the subsequent proposals of the Grimond Review Body (page 123). For instance, the students renounced any claim to be represented at Senate.

The centre-stone of the 3 MeV Dynamitron accelerator, main component of the Radiation Centre, was set in position jointly by (ABOVE) the Vice-Chancellor, Dr R B Hunter (with hammer) and Dr J A Pope, Vice-Chancellor of the new University of Aston in Birmingham. The Centre was opened in 1972, for joint use by the two Universities, by Sir Alan Cottrell, former student and Professor of Physical Metallurgy, Chief Scientific Adviser to the Government.

RIGHT: The Dynamitron rectifier stack and corona rings. The Centre contains other radiation sources and associated laboratories for use by chemists, physicists, biologists and others, with suction tube transmission system for irradiated specimens.

Members of the Review Body which was set up by the University Council in January 1971 under the chairmanship of the Rt Hon Jo Grimond, MP to "consider the role, constitution and functioning of the University of Birmingham and to make recommendations to Council for any desirable changes".

Front, L to R : Professor Dorothy Hodgkin, Chancellor of the University of Bristol; Professor the Rev Canon J G Davies, Head of the Department of Theology; Mr Grimond; J R Jarvis, Senior Research Associate; Charles P Thompson, Bursar; Carolyn Sparkes, biology student, who graduated with first class honours while serving on the Review Body.

BACK: Rodney G Playford, President of the Guild of Students 1970-71; Dr Alan Macey, Guild of Graduates; Sir Maurice Dean (Secretary); Sir Peter Venables, Pro-Chancellor of the Open University and first Vice-Chancellor of the University of Aston; Sir Stephen F Burman, Pro-Chancellor 1955-66.
    Absent: Dr Peter H Davison, Non-professorial Staff.

The Review Body took evidence from all sections of the campus, and gathered for occasional weekend meetings at a Banbury hotel where this photograph was taken. Its final report was presented in September 1972. Most of the Council's consequent proposals have been implemented, apart from those requiring Privy Council approval.
    The main change in the administrative structure—transfer of supreme power from the Court of Governors to the Council—was approved by the Court itself; but the proposal that Council should acquire an academic majority and constitute a single authority in academic as well as lay matters was rejected.
    The Grimond proposals for representation of students and non-professorial staff in the University government were broadly accepted. They include substantially increased representation on Senate and Faculty boards. The authority of heads of departments is now limited by mandatory departmental committees.

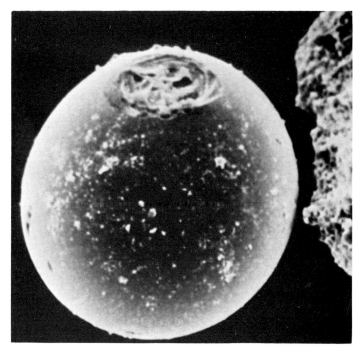

From the moon to the garden plot. These two pages are no more than a token of the immense research programmes in which the University is engaged. Spending from research grants and contracts has now exceeded £3½m in a single year. It touches upon cancer and deafness, atomic power, outer space, the nature of matter, industrial production, new materials, the workings of the law, the secrets of Byzantium, road accidents, the common potato, town planning, games of chance, recycling of waste products, pollution, local government, communications in 2000 AD—to mention but a few subjects chosen at random.

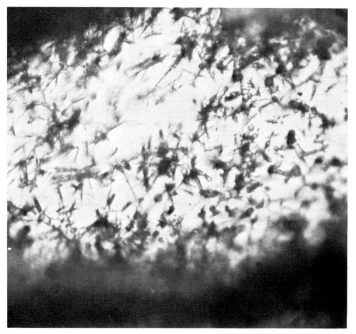

Research on moon rocks, from both American and Russian missions, has been in progress since 1971 under the direction of Dr S A Durrani. The pictures show an Apollo 15 lunar glass spherule (TOP RIGHT), a third of a millimetre in diameter, which has been 'chipped' by the impact of a cosmic-dust particle such as the one shown TOP LEFT (an iron micrometeorite, a thousandth of a millimetre in size) sitting in its own microcrater. A successful laboratory simulation of this rare capture, using the Department of Space Research 'dust accelerator' is seen BOTTOM LEFT.

BOTTOM RIGHT: a photomicrograph of cosmic-ray tracks in a lunar pyroxene crystal, appropriately etched, and viewed through an optical microscope.

124

In 1965 a Government committee under Professor Harry Thorpe, Head of the Department of Geography, began probing the future of allotments. Its published conclusion (HMSO Cmnd 4166) was that they should be retained, no longer as a source of cheap vegetables for the 'labouring poor' but as a worthwhile form of recreation, under the new title of Leisure Gardens, with facilities for all the family.

Between World War II and 1965 the number of plots had fallen from 1,450,000 to 635,000, of which many lay derelict. The Report has led to a revival. Many authorities are now following its suggestions that sites should be attractively laid out, with hard-surfaced roads, pathways, car parks, piped water, WCs, a pavilion and a storeshed, and that tenants should be encouraged to erect their own small summerhouses.

The first site (detail above) at Westwood Heath, Coventry, was opened in 1971. The layout sketch shows wedge-shaped plots grouped round a footway system, segregated from roads and car parking. Further research in the Department has centred on Birmingham allotments, with Social Science Research Council support, and on European systems.

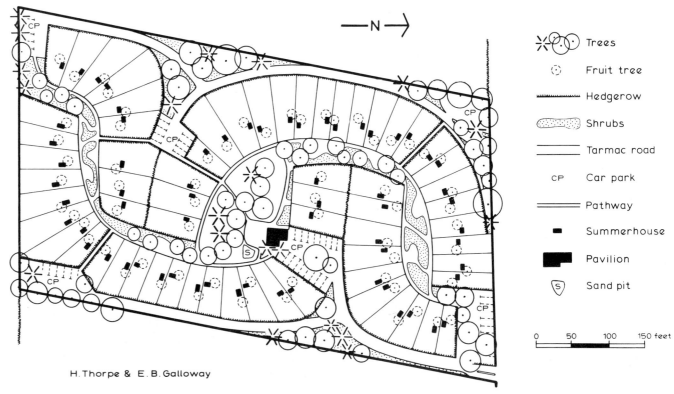

— N —→

☼⚬⚬⚬⦁	Trees
⦿	Fruit tree
	Hedgerow
⬡	Shrubs
═══	Tarmac road
CP	Car park
═══	Pathway
▪	Summerhouse
◼	Pavilion
Ⓢ	Sand pit

0   50   100   150 feet

H. Thorpe & E. B. Galloway

LEFT: Edward Heath was Prime Minister when he visited the University in February 1973. He is seen here with (L to R) Sir George Farmer (Pro-Chancellor), Professor Hamish Miles (Director, Barber Institute) and J D Medley (Chairman, Barber Trust). Behind the Pro-Chancellor is W R G Lewis (Registrar, full face) talking with Professor O Hood Phillips (Pro-Vice-Chancellor).

BELOW: Architect's sketch of the new Lucas Institute for Engineering Production in Edgbaston Park Road, which was formally opened in June 1973 by Sir Kenneth Corley, Chairman of Joseph Lucas. The company had again made a substantial contribution. The building combines hotel facilities with lecture rooms for business executives attending short courses at the Institute.

RIGHT: The University's international reputation in Byzantine studies is enhanced by an annual spring symposium. At the seventh of these in 1973 there was the first performance for a thousand years of the Game of the 19 Beds, a favourite entertainment performed by gothic dancers (BELOW) for the Emperor Constantine VII and his Empress (ABOVE).

FAR RIGHT: A contrast in student common rooms. The Mason Lounge in the new Arts Building and (BELOW) Founder's Room at Edmund Street in 1960, just before the final move to Edgbaston.

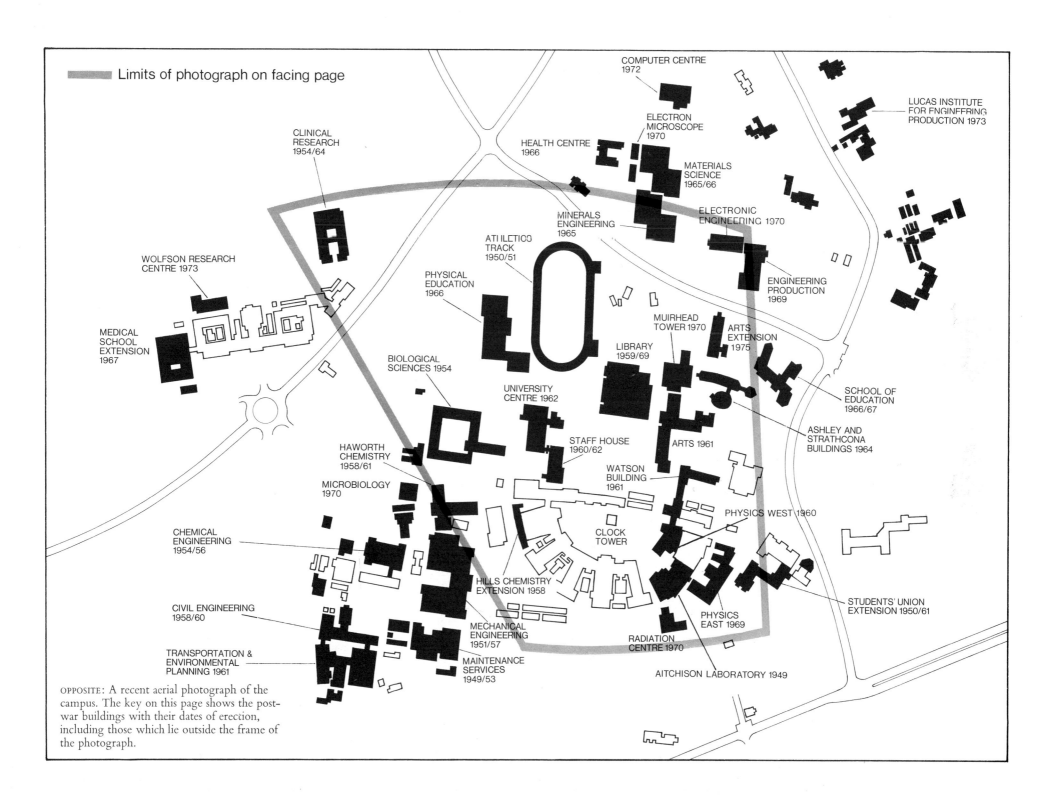

Limits of photograph on facing page

COMPUTER CENTRE 1972

LUCAS INSTITUTE FOR ENGINEERING PRODUCTION 1973

ELECTRON MICROSCOPE 1970

HEALTH CENTRE 1966

CLINICAL RESEARCH 1954/64

MATERIALS SCIENCE 1965/66

ELECTRONIC ENGINEERING 1970

MINERALS ENGINEERING 1965

ATHLETICS TRACK 1950/51

WOLFSON RESEARCH CENTRE 1973

PHYSICAL EDUCATION 1966

ENGINEERING PRODUCTION 1969

MUIRHEAD TOWER 1970

ARTS EXTENSION 1975

LIBRARY 1959/69

MEDICAL SCHOOL EXTENSION 1967

BIOLOGICAL SCIENCES 1954

UNIVERSITY CENTRE 1962

SCHOOL OF EDUCATION 1966/67

ASHLEY AND STRATHCONA BUILDINGS 1964

STAFF HOUSE 1960/62

ARTS 1961

HAWORTH CHEMISTRY 1958/61

WATSON BUILDING 1961

MICROBIOLOGY 1970

PHYSICS WEST 1960

CHEMICAL ENGINEERING 1954/56

CLOCK TOWER

HILLS CHEMISTRY EXTENSION 1958

STUDENTS' UNION EXTENSION 1950/61

CIVIL ENGINEERING 1958/60

PHYSICS EAST 1969

TRANSPORTATION & ENVIRONMENTAL PLANNING 1961

MECHANICAL ENGINEERING 1951/57

RADIATION CENTRE 1970

MAINTENANCE SERVICES 1949/53

AITCHISON LABORATORY 1949

OPPOSITE: A recent aerial photograph of the campus. The key on this page shows the post-war buildings with their dates of erection, including those which lie outside the frame of the photograph.

Towards the end of his period as Chancellor Lord Avon came to name the Muirhead Tower after J H Muirhead, Professor of Philosophy 1897-1921. He is seen LEFT with (L to R) Anne Naylor (President of the Guild of Students 1971-72), Rod Playford (past President and member of the Review Body) and Paul Dodgson (Vice-President). Soon afterwards Lord Avon announced his intention of retiring.

His successor, Sir Peter Scott, is seen ABOVE, with the Vice-Chancellor after his installation in May 1974, when he conferred honorary degrees on four men who had been closely associated with him in his work for the protection of the environment and the conservation of wild life—Maurice Strong (Director of the UN Environment Programme), Sir Landsborough Thomson, Professor Konrad Lorenz and Sir Herbert Bonar.

Sir Peter described himself as "a somewhat off-beat Chancellor". Soon after his installation he spent a day sailing (RIGHT) and gliding with the two student clubs. He is the University's third personal link—after D G Lillie and Sir Raymond Priestley—with his father, Scott of the Antarctic.

Upon the foundations laid by Sir Raymond Priestley the University established a leading position in sport and physical education.

FAR LEFT TOP: At a dinner given in 1970 to honour athletes who had competed in the Commonwealth Games that year are (L to R) Howard Payne, lecturer in Physical Education (gold medal, hammer throw); his wife Rosemary (gold, discus); the Vice-Chancellor, Dr R B Hunter; the Pro-Chancellor, Sir George Farmer; Ian Hallam, dental student (gold, 400m cycling persuit). A bronze was also won by Kevan Moran, student, in swimming.

FAR LEFT, BOTTOM: Mike Jones, medical student, who in 1972 became the first canoeist to navigate the 200 miles of the Blue Nile below Lake Tana. He was helped by three companions and a £1,000 Churchill Scholarship.

LEFT: Instruction in the use of aqualung equipment for students at the University's site on Lake Coniston, where an outdoor centre is being built as a memorial to Sir Raymond Priestley.

ABOVE AND RIGHT: A contrast in styles—the 1926-27 netball team, and tennis players in the new Sports Centre.

Participation in physical activity has ceased to be compulsory for first year students, but the great majority participate voluntarily. One reason is the very wide range of choice offered, which includes judo, sub-aqua, fencing, horse riding, sailing and different forms of dance, as well as the traditional sports.

The annual students' carnival began in 1921 as "The Birmingham University Hospital Carnival." After the coming of the National Health Service its proceeds were diverted to the needs of the young, the old and the handicapped in and around Birmingham.

The standard recipe was a procession through the streets on a Saturday in October accompanied by a horde of students shaking collecting boxes. A typical 'float' entered by the History Students' Fellowship in 1925 is seen left.

The event reached a peak of success in the 1950s with nett proceeds rising to £15,000, helped by a carnival ball which achieved a high level of social acceptability. Picture TOP RIGHT shows the 1950 carnival chairman Max Feeny (now a Recorder on the Northern Circuit) with the carnival queen, Kathleen O'Donnell, and on his right the 1947 queen, Violet Pretty—better known as the film actress Anne Heywood.

The lower picture shows the busy carnival office of that year. The student with the pipe is Leslie Brent, now Professor of Immunology at St. Marys Hospital, London.

Recent years have seen a sharp drop in the Carnival's fortunes. In 1960 the University moved the date from October to June; in 1961 the proceeds dropped to £4,000 and never recovered. The date was moved to March when it became a joint effort with the University of Aston, but the deterioration continued. In 1975 the total raised by street collection was £156, compared with £3,960 in 1927. Plans for moving the date to November are now in hand.

FAR RIGHT: This giant effigy of Brian from BBC TV's *Magic Roundabout* is one of the many elaborate mockups devised for recent carnivals.

In a 1970 carnival stunt the Clock Tower was scaled (LEFT) by a member of the University Mountaineering Club, Chris Perry, a postgraduate in Civil Engineering, now in America. He did it with professional caution, using two ropes and a two-way walkie-talkie. The 280 ft climb to the parapet took half an hour, and success was signalled by a special chime of the clock bell.

BELOW: In 1965 a nautical tandem was ridden across the English Channel in 8 hrs 55 min by two Chemical Engineering students, Ron Brooks (FRONT) and Jim Wood, seen here with their craft at Gas Street Basin, Birmingham.

Though sartorially out of fashion, the straw boater remains correct dress for a bit of light-hearted fun. LEFT: A moment during the Jubilee celebrations in 1950. ABOVE: The Columbus Society on an outing to Stratford-upon-Avon. The Society claims to be open to all students having "a mental age of between 4 and 8"; most of its members help back-stage with Guild Theatre Group productions. It is sometimes confused with the Society for the Abolition of Thursday Nights, which organises group outings for the sole purpose of enjoyment.

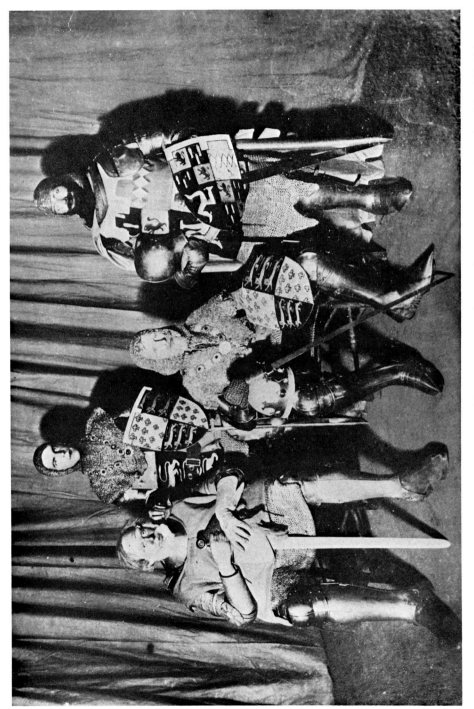

Stage presentations have been a strong feature of University life since Mason College days. After the 1911 production of *Henry IV* (above) Oxford University nearly lost a future Merton Professor of English when F P Wilson, who played Falstaff, was persuaded by John Drinkwater to tour the Midlands with the Pilgrim Players. Fortunately for Oxford he declined the subsequent offer of a job with Birmingham Repertory Company.

BELOW: The cast of *Young Person In Pink*, produced in 1922-23 by University House. Wearing her grandmother's bonnet is Miss Alice Godsell, a chemistry graduate who began her working life as personal assistant to the Director of the Chemical Research Laboratory at Teddington, Sir Gilbert Morgan, former Mason Professor of Chemistry. The dramatic tradition in University House began with Margery Fry.

RUGBY INTERNATIONALS
TO-DAY : By D. R. GENT.
Page 13.

DAILY GRAPHIC
SATURDAY, FEBRUARY 27, 1926.

FACES AND FROCKS.
By K. R. G. BROWNE.
Page 7.

Next Week's Production of "Salma" by Birmingham Students.

Members of Birmingham University Dramatic Society rehearsing "Salma," by L. Cranmer-Byng, which they are to perform at the Midland Institute Theatre next week. "Salma" is "a drama of April played in Cintra, 1,000 years ago." Professor Granville Bantock has composed the music for the production.

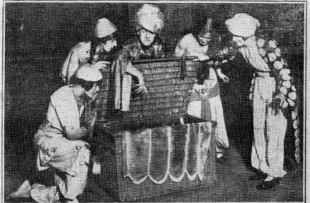

Abu'l Fath the Jester (E. A. Knight) and the ladies of the harim in a scene "in the Harim of the Wali in the Palace of Cintra."

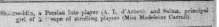

Shamsuddin, a Persian lute player (A. L. d'Arbeu) and Salma, principal girl of a troupe of strolling players (Miss Madeleine Carroll).

Omar Ibn Said, Wali of Cintra (H. W. Burdett), and Tahir, his Comptroller (C. J. Ward).

The... of the orchestra, who are all students —Miss Christina Smye and Miss Edna de Lacy Ross.

Printed and Published by GRAPHIC PUBLICATIONS, LIMITED, at Graphic Buildings, Whitefriars, in the City of London—Saturday, February 27, 1926. Sole Agents for South Africa: Central News Agency, Ltd.

In 1926 Birmingham University Dramatic Society presented another now-forgotten play called *Salma* by Captain Cranmer-Byng. It had incidental music composed by Granville Bantock and conducted by Adrian Boult. This was the era of local 'slip pages' in the national press; on the left is one of two which the Daily Graphic published.

The leads were played by film actress Madeleine Carroll, then a student in French, and Alphonso ('Pon') d'Abreu, now Emeritus Professor of Surgery, who provided these mementos.

Anthony Eden, future Chancellor, made his first appearance on the University scene; he came with a party from Warwick Castle led by Basil Dean, the impresario.

Drama and Theatre Arts became a separate department offering its own honours course in 1964, and for the first ten places within the Combined Subjects degree it received 233 applications.

LEFT: Students of the Drama Department produced *The Foursome* by E A Whitehead in 1972 with (L to R) Jane Wymark, Nick Hughes, Bill Lloyd and Lynn Purnell.

ABOVE AND RIGHT: Scenes from Carl Orff's *Carmina Burana*, a fully choreographed version of which was performed in the Great Hall in 1974 by the City of Birmingham Symphony Orchestra conducted by Professor Ivor Keys. Jane Winearls, the first lecturer in dance to be appointed by a University in this country, did the choreography. The choir of two hundred were mainly students.

The Queen came in 1975 to open the Mason College Centenary Exhibition in the Library. LEFT: Her Majesty stops to talk with members of the large crowd in University Square during her walk from the Library to Staff House.

ABOVE: With Dr Kenneth W Humphreys, Librarian since 1952, whose appointment as the first Librarian of the new European University Institute at Florence had recently been announced.

Our title explained. The mermaid with mirror and comb was Sir Josiah Mason's heraldic crest, borrowed from an earlier and apparently unrelated Mason of Greenwich—without authority, according to Fox-Davies's *Complete Guide to Heraldry*. She thus found her way into the Mason College badge (ABOVE) and the University Coat of Arms. She was evidently as much an object of affection to Mason as she has been to a century of students, for her figure in stone perched on the pinnacle of Mason College and remained there for 85 years; she was then rescued and re-erected, minus arms, in the foyer of the Students' Union where she now is (LEFT). There is another version set into the floor of the foyer, a third on the fountain outside (RIGHT) and a fourth (superimposed, RIGHT) on the Union extension.

Her name has been attached to journals and sporting clubs, and she is currently the symbol of a research project in irradiation of the human body being conducted jointly by the Medical School and the Department of Physics.

The editors of an earlier Mermaid magazine poured out a stream of extravagant metaphors and similes in her name—"Mistress of the caves of foam". . . "erect on the rock from which she is going to plunge she pauses". . . and so forth.

Long may she reign.

Sketch by Helen Jones, of the City Engineer's
Department, showing where Mason College
stood in relation to the new City Library.